£2

Life Is a Road Trip!

A Journey into Mindfulness

KAREN DAVEY-WINTER

ISBN: 978-0-9898-1930-5 (sc)
ISBN: 978-0-9898-1931-2 (e)

Library of Congress Control Number: 2013920794

Lulu Publishing Services rev. date: 11/25/2013

For Joshua

With all my love, always.

Contents

Introduction

"It is in your moments of decision that your destiny is shaped." – Anthony Robbins[1]

I have made some of my biggest decisions on the road. Seventeen years ago, I was stuck in traffic on my way to work on the M25 in South London, desperately trying to figure out what I could do to change my life. My job was a poor fit, and I had a miserable commute. As the traffic ground to a halt and the highway resembled a parking lot, a million ideas went through my mind. Should I move back to Australia? Should I travel around the world for a year? Should I move to America? I pondered the latter idea for the remaining hour I was in traffic, and I made up my mind. I walked into the office and told a colleague what I'd decided. Two months later I moved to San Francisco, California, and I have never looked back. What began as a one-hour commute from South London to Egham became a life-changing journey.

When I made the decision to have a child on my own, it wasn't even close to a one-hour journey. It was just a ten-minute drive home after another dreadful first date. I resolved then that I wasn't going to continue searching for the man of my dreams. There was no assurance that I would find him before I turned forty, but I did know that by the time I turned forty I might no longer be able to have children. I didn't want to reach that point and look back with regret and longing. So I decided to do it on my own. On April 1, 2002, at 12:34 p.m., my son, Joshua, was born. He is the light of my life, my favorite person in the world. Nothing in my life makes me feel more proud.

I don't remember exactly when Josh and I decided to take the road trip I describe in this book, so I'm guessing we weren't in the car. But however we decided, at the start of 2012 I found myself saving money so that I could take eight weeks off and drive around the United States. In January 2012, I started doing what I do best. I created a timeline and put together a spreadsheet – with multiple tabs. No, really. I'm organized, I like things to be in their place, and I like creating structure. It has served me well in almost every area of my life. I'm also very good at it.

I briefly contemplated finding hotels along the way and trying to be more spontaneous than I typically am. But a quick look at the cost of staying in some of the national parks on our list (Yosemite, Yellowstone, Mount Rushmore) revealed the cheapest places would be at least $200 a night. So spontaneity went out the window, and I called the reservation service before those $200 options were no longer available.

I then started thinking about visits along the way with good friends in North Carolina, New Mexico, California and Washington states. I started contacting them, hoping I wasn't planning too early. Everyone was excited to have us stay, and before I knew it, I had anchored us in specific places at specific times. My spreadsheet was filling up. Once I had a basic structure in place, it felt risky not to finish it. If I didn't cover a certain amount of distance between the visits, the schedule would be jeopardized and we might not get back home in time.

By the middle of February, I had a detailed spreadsheet with dates and locations, ideas for activities we could do in each place, and a budget forecast, including contingencies. The trip had a shape, and the logistics were finalized. The decision to take a road trip was now backed up by a plan with a schedule. We were ready for our journey.

~ఎ~

"The ability to make effective choices and live an authentic life depends to a great extent on a capacity to be self reflective." – James W. Tamm[2]

My friends and family had varied reactions when I told them I was planning this trip. Some thought it was exciting; others thought it was daring, slightly unusual, and perhaps even a little irresponsible. As we sat around my sister's kitchen table in England in the spring of 2012, I described the places that we would visit and the details in my spreadsheet. I said I was planning to write a book with a theme for each week, something we would pay attention to as we traveled. It would be a project in mindfulness. My brother-in-law, only half jokingly, ribbed me about my plan. "So let's see, you've turned what could be a very spontaneous, off-the-wall trip into a project . . . how very like you!"

I laughed. Well, yes, I had. I reflected on that briefly and realized he was right. I have a bias to action, and I'd acted. I had organized the trip and decided I would write a book. I was moving forward. The ideas for the book grew, and I identified a theme for each week. There was no real design to them, with the exception of Freedom for the first week, because I was thinking of freedom from work, and Gratitude for the last week, because I knew I would feel grateful for the trip. I chose themes that I'm curious about, that show up frequently in my work as a coach and consultant, and that I'm still learning about. I decided I would send out an e-mail to my friends, clients and colleagues every week to solicit their input. Just as the logistics of our trip were taking shape, the book and our mindfulness project was evolving, and the journey was beginning.

I wondered what big decision I would make on this trip. But as time went by, I realized this trip wasn't about making decisions. It was about reflection – something I'm not especially good at, so there was a lot for me to learn. This trip was about my ability to pay attention, using different lenses to learn how to process life in new ways. At times it was uncomfortable. But I found I had different choices when I was mindful, and I observed how that led to different results.

⟡

> "When you are moving toward an objective . . . it is very important to pay attention to the road. It is the road that teaches us the best way to get there, and the road enriches us as we walk its length." – Paulo Coehlo[3]

The night before we left, I sent out the first e-mail asking for input on freedom, suggesting the following questions:

- What does freedom mean to you?
- What does it look like, sound like, feel like?
- When are you at your most free?
- What stands in the way of freedom?

I did the same thing at the start of every week, with similar questions about each new theme. The responses provided critical input to this book. People's insights and feedback helped me look at things differently and created an often enlightening source of conversation with Josh, who would listen as I read the e-mail replies out loud.

As the weeks went by, it became clear that one way of improving something is to simply pay attention to it. When you notice your reactions and learn what it tells you about yourself, you can try something different the next time. Then you can pay attention to that and see if there is more to learn. The themes also became intertwined.

- Freedom – The focus in our first week gave us the space to open up our minds to new ways of doing and being. The ability to start thinking of ourselves as free had a strong influence and led us directly into the theme of our second week.
- Impact – This week we noticed the effect we had on others. We also paid attention to what the impact of situations and other people told us about ourselves.
- Kindness – In the third week, we noticed that when people showed us kindness the outcome was uplifting. When we showed kindness to others, it increased our connection.
- Connection – With this theme came a sense of belonging. We connected to memories, familiar places, and, perhaps most of all, to each other. We even learned how to sustain a connection through difficult conversations.
- Empathy – When we practiced empathy we understood each other better, and our connection increased again.
- Collaboration – Taking the trouble to understand people's interests, strengths, and contributions improved our experiences. What we learned about empathy helped us by making it easier to see another person's point of view.
- Curiosity – This prompted us to ask more questions and gather more information. It also improved our connection to each other and with others.

- Gratitude – This surrounded everything in our final week, making us feel happier and increasing our ability to be kind, show empathy, collaborate, connect, and be curious.

By the end of the trip, I learned that paying attention to something improves our awareness of it. This increased mindfulness results in the ability to make a different choice about how we approach a given situation. When we make a different choice, with intention rather than reaction, we get a better outcome. We have the opportunity to learn, try new approaches, and realize that often our own judgments get in the way of the result we want. When we show ourselves compassion for those judgments, they become a more integrated part of who we are, and we start to live more authentically. After eight weeks, our trip was over. But through this journey of mindfulness and new choices, I increased my understanding and gained self-awareness. In doing this I found a new level of self-acceptance. The trip was over, but my journey was still underway.

A NOTE TO THE READER

This book is a coaching journey, juxtaposed against the stories of our trip. It is intended to help you look at your life in new ways and gain different perspectives. It will help you overcome the obstacles that are preventing you from living the life you want. As a result, you will see better outcomes in various areas of your life – as a parent, partner, friend, co-worker, and leader. If you want to make meaningful changes in your life and are a lifelong learner, this book is for you.

Each chapter contains exercises with an action and reflection component. These were designed with the following context:

- Reflection – many of us typically respond to life in "action" mode, and I'm certainly no exception. But this trip was a time of reflection, so many of the exercises start with a question to guide reflection.

- Action – In some cases, the action comes first, because it is required in order to reflect on the theme. And for my son, Josh, the trip was all about the action!

Each exercise is designed to make you think about an aspect of the theme differently or to try something new and see what happens. The questions dig deep so that you will learn from the exercise.

The following are a few suggestions about how to approach reading the book and doing the exercises:

- Simply read the book as a story, reflecting on themes as you read through, but without writing notes or practicing the exercises. You will learn from this approach, but not as much as you would if you took one of the following approaches.
- Read a chapter per week (or whatever time period is feasible) and take time to absorb the theme. Practice the exercises and notice what comes up when you're being mindful. Each exercise is also included separately at the end with a space to write notes. The learning in this method will be deeper.
- Take the above approach, but post your results on my blog (http://worklifeperspectives.com/Life_is_a_Road_Trip_.html), as well as writing notes. The learning here will be even deeper. By taking the extra step to share what you learned, you will gain the benefit of reading what others have learned and perhaps find resonance with comments on the themes you enjoyed.

However you decide to use this book, I hope you enjoy it. The model of paying attention to a theme can be used in any context – your personal life, your work, or your relationships. It doesn't need to be limited to the themes in this book; it could be any theme about which you want to know more, in any area of your life you want to improve. In the Afterword section at the end of the book, I will give you some ideas of how to create your own mindfulness project.

This book is part of my life journey, both physically and metaphorically. The hardest part of my journey relates to self-acceptance, and practicing mindfulness helped move me forward. The hardest part of your journey might be different. Taking the model and using it in your own context will make it about your journey, your mindfulness, and your choices. And I hope it becomes a rich part of your life journey.

Josh's Journal

Week 1

June 22nd, 2012
Drove to see JanJan. Today was long!

June 23rd, 2012
I went hiking to see some big waterfalls.

June 24th, 2012
I went on and drove a four-wheeler. It was amazing!

June 25th, 2012
Today I went to the Falcons Stadium, the headquarters
for Coke and last I went and saw my Mom's friends for
dinner. Today was awesome!

June 26th, 2012
I saw Bourbon Street and the Battleship USS Alabama.
Today was nice.

June 27th, 2012
I went on a ferry to the Battle of Chalmette. Today was
great.

Freedom

Week 1: San Antonio, Texas; via Hendersonville, North Carolina; Atlanta, Georgia; and New Orleans, Louisiana.

Total mileage so far: 1,790.

Theme for Week 1: Freedom.

"Freedom is the last, best hope of Earth."[4] - Abraham Lincoln

The last time I took eight weeks off work was when I moved to California in 1996, so as we got in the car at 8:00 a.m. on Friday, June 22, 2012, I felt a mixture of excitement and trepidation. I was excited to be free of the logistics of daily life, the schedule driven by the need to earn a living and to arrive at my son's soccer games on time. It was thrilling to be able to decide what I wanted to do each day and not be driven by what I needed to do for the sake of someone else. But I felt trepidation because eight weeks without pay is a long time and more than 8,500 miles is a long way to travel as the sole driver. For the next eight weeks, life would be both flexible and uncertain.

> *"I almost always associate freedom with the ability to jump in a car and drive anywhere I want."*
>
> *Abby, Australia*

As we drove out of our neighborhood, I reminded Josh of our theme for Week 1: Freedom.

Karen: When we get to the end of the week, I will ask you to summarize what you think about freedom.
Josh: Freedom is about letting go and doing what you want to do.

Karen: That's fabulous, Josh, I'm going to write that down.
Josh: Well it is. It's about letting go, no one can tell you what to do; it's about being yourself. It's not that hard Mom . . .

Throughout the week it would become clear that he was right. Freedom was about the choice to do what we wanted, the opportunity to try new things, and the chance to learn

> *"I think to me, freedom is about having the choice of how you spend your time and who with."*
>
> *Alex, England*

from the results. It was about being who we are and the freedom to accept ourselves. We also learned that there are things that get in the way of freedom. Sometimes we put these roadblocks in our own way; other times they are beyond our control. Taking this trip gave us space to investigate what happens when you pay attention to life in a different way. Reflecting on freedom in the first week gave us the foundation to contemplate the themes in the remaining seven weeks of our trip. It made us aware of choice, how we can always choose to do something different, and the consequences of our choices. It also started a journey of learning that has been invaluable for both of us.

❧

"Freedom is, first of all, the chance to formulate the available choices, to argue over them and then, the opportunity to choose." – C. Wright Mills[5]

Initially it seemed simple. Obviously we wanted to be free. However, it turned out that freedom is more complex than that. When I planned the trip, I was excited to have so many options for how to spend each day of the next eight weeks. However, I created a multi-tab spreadsheet, pre-booked the hotels, and planned visits with friends. Once I'd put this structure in place, there was constraint and less room for spontaneous choice. What a paradox. Even though I could have changed most of the hotel bookings, there was a potential domino effect on the overall schedule and our ability to get back home in time.

So even though at its core, freedom is about the ability to choose, once a choice is made there are consequences, and sometimes those consequences result in constraints on freedom. Michael Welp said, "Polarities are interdependent opposites which function best when both are present to balance with the other."[6] Throughout the trip we moved in and out of freedom and constraint, like a figure eight going around a polarity map.

> *"I think there is a certain limitation on freedom once you have committed to something that is a priority over your freedom."*
>
> Ann, California, USA

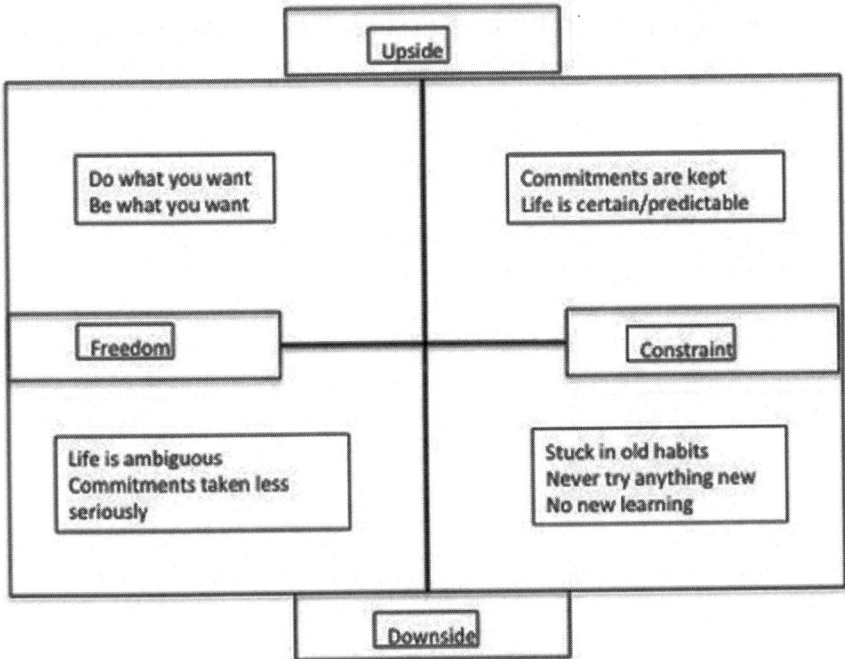

The polarity map shows some of the complexity implicit in freedom, the choices we make, and the consequences of those choices. Moving around the polarity map changes the balance of the polar opposites, the balance between freedom and constraint. It also changes the consequences.

ACTION: Create a polarity map of your own. Choose a theme in your life – like freedom – that involves your biggest challenge or the thing that you most desire. Identify the polar opposites and enter them in the middle two boxes. Fill in the four squares with the upsides and downsides of each polarity. Locate yourself on the map and mark that place with an X.

REFLECTION: Reflect on where you are in the map. Is that where you want to be? If not, identify where you want to be with a Y on the map. How will you get there? What will the outcome of moving to Y be?

You may complete this exercise and all the exercises in the chapter in the exercise section at the back of the book and share your observations on my blog at: http://worklifeperspectives.com/Life_is_a_Road_Trip_.html

✑

"What then is freedom? The power to live as one wishes."[7]
- Marcus Tillius Cicero

The first stop on our trip was with my great friend Janice in North Carolina and her partner, Nita. Janice and I have known each other since 1986, when we worked as waitresses in Myrtle Beach, South Carolina. I was there on an exchange program from Manchester University in the UK; she was on summer break from the University of North Carolina.

Though friends, our approach to life is different. I am organized and know what I'm doing days, weeks, and often months in advance. Conversely, Janice has a vague idea what her day might look like, but her plans are just a framework and can be changed at any time. I told her I planned to write a book about our trip, with different themes every week. When I said I chose the theme of Freedom for the first week with the idea that I would be free from a schedule, she laughed out loud. I looked at her, not sure what I had said that was so funny. She said, "You will *never* be free from a schedule."

Well, Janice was right. But I thought, *"At least this is my schedule, and therefore my choice!"*

Josh loves staying with Janice. He loves that we're not tied to a plan and that we make it up as we go along. The day after we arrived, I asked him to get dressed for hiking. His response was, "Mom, I'm on Appalachian time." I took a breath and realized that I didn't need to do what I always do. I didn't need to organize or start thinking about the next thing we were going to do. I, too, could relax. I, too, could get on Appalachian time. That's not natural for me, and that's why it was important that I try it. That's why Janice is my friend and why this was the first stop on our trip. I had something to learn.

For the next two days, we hiked in the mountains where *The Hunger Games* was made, visited Lake Lure, where key scenes from *Dirty Dancing* were filmed, and dropped in unexpectedly on Janice's sister. We stayed up late, and we relaxed. The mountains were beautiful. By virtue of being with someone very different from me, in a place very different from my home, I made the choice to slow down, go with the flow, and be spontaneous and adaptable. I had the freedom to experience something different, and I paid attention to the results. I felt lighter, like someone had taken away some of my responsibilities. It was uplifting.

Choosing an approach that works best for a given situation, even if it's uncomfortable, improves the chances of a better outcome. As we drove away from North Carolina, I reflected on the lessons I had learned. What serves us well in one aspect of life doesn't always serve us best in another. The structure that I apply to my life works well in the majority of situations I deal with: Juggling the demands of a single parent, organizing projects at work, coordinating trips to the UK to visit my family. But if I'd arrived at Janice's house and tried to put us on a schedule for the entire weekend, I would have not only failed miserably and frustrated myself, but I also would have driven Janice, Nita, and Josh crazy. Giving up my tendency to create structure, when it was not needed, resulted in a feeling of freedom that I decided to enjoy.

Despite that lesson, I felt just a tiny bit relieved as we pulled out of Janice's driveway and headed toward Atlanta. I felt at ease as I returned to my schedule. It was illuminating to experience someone else's approach to life, and it gave me a taste of what the theme of Empathy would feel like later in the trip. But it was comforting to be back in control, knowing the structure of my day. As James Tamm says in his excellent book *Radical Collaboration*, "Our preferences don't cause problems for us; it is our inability to be flexible in circumstances that call for an approach different from our preference that creates a problem."[8]

> **REFLECTION**: What is your typical approach to life? Are you organized, flexible, spontaneous, structured? Think of some situations and identify the most consistent patterns for you.

> **ACTION**: Choose a situation and identify the opposite approach. If you are normally structured, try being flexible. If you are normally organized, try being spontaneous. What happens? How does it feel? What did you learn about yourself?

⤸

"A true friend is someone who lets you have total freedom to be yourself."[9] - Jim Morrison

As we drove toward Atlanta, Josh was most excited to tour the Georgia Dome football stadium, where the Atlanta Falcons play. I was looking forward to be seeing my friend Catherine, whom I hadn't seen since Josh and I left California in 2004. Catherine has a special place in my heart because she looked after Josh for a few months after he was born while I returned to work. The three of us met at the stadium, took the tour, and then raced from one end of the field to the other. We then toured World of Coca-Cola, enjoying the soda memorabilia and tasting as many of the sixty different Coke products from around the world as we could stomach.

Later, as we relaxed at the hotel before dinner, Catherine and I updated each other on the changes in our lives during the last eight years. She had gotten divorced, lived in Amsterdam, moved back to Atlanta, changed jobs, and set up her own consulting business. I'd moved to the

> *"When I feel the most free in my life is when I can make decisions to be who I want to, to be a good person and respect others, to have a dream and chase that dream."*
> *Antonio, California, USA*

East Coast, changed jobs, moved in with someone, moved on from that relationship, changed careers, and set up my own coaching and consulting business. We had both been busy.

I felt freedom in that moment of sharing. I knew that she would understand and not judge, and she felt the same safety with me. We knew that we would still be accepted for who we are. For me, being in the vulnerable place of admitting that I'd made some bad decisions out of a deep-seated desire to be loved was both uncomfortable and freeing. In her powerful book *The Gifts of Imperfection*, Brené Brown talks about vulnerability, the courage it takes to share our stories, and the innate longing we all have for connection. "When we're looking for compassion . . . we need someone who embraces us for our strengths and struggles."[10]

Later that week, as Josh and I we were coming back from a boat tour of Chalmette in New Orleans, our conversation about freedom changed.

Josh: So how is your book going?
Karen: Pretty good – I'm just writing notes at the moment.
Josh: I think freedom is just about being yourself.
Karen: Do you feel able to be yourself?
Josh: Sometimes . . .
I worried that at the age of 10 he already felt like he couldn't always be himself.
Karen: So when you say "sometimes," what can I do to help you feel more yourself more often?
Josh: Nothing really, it's all down to me. It's really about school. I don't feel as free at school because I have to do things I don't want to do. I mean, PE is fine, but I wish there was a device you could put in your brain and learn everything you need to know in three minutes, then you could do what you want . . .

I had known I was free to be myself with Catherine. And intuitively Josh already knew there are some people with whom he felt less free to truly be himself.

REFLECTION: With whom and in what situation do you feel most free to be yourself? With whom and in what situation do you feel least able to be yourself? Why is that?

7

ACTION: Next time you are with the person that least enables you to be yourself, make a note of what happens. What do you notice about your relationship with that person? What did you learn about yourself?

⳥

"You gain strength, courage and confidence by every experience in which you stop to look fear in the face."[11] - Eleanor Roosevelt

So what gets in the way of freedom?

When we were in Lake Lure, we wandered around the shops, looking at all the tourist knick-knacks. I used my credit card to pay for a fishing rod and some water shoes for Josh, and the store clerk asked to see my identification. I opened the place in my wallet where I keep my license, and all I saw was my expired California license, not my current Maryland license. Horror washed over me.

> *"When I think about it most of the shackles are put upon us by our own or someone else's expectations."*
>
> *Liz, England*

Immediately I realized where it was. In my effort to be organized, I decided to take a copy of my driver's license and put it in the spare wheel section of my car (along with a spare credit card and car key) in case I should lose my handbag at some point on the trip. I had made the copy by scanning it on my home printer. My driver's license was still on the printer glass.

Carrying your driver's license is required by law in America. I was about to drive more than 8,500 miles around the country, I was on day three of fifty-six, and my driver's license was at home. The self-judgment monologue in my head went loudly down a negative spiral:

- *Oh my god, I'm such an idiot – any other time it wouldn't matter but to be without my license for EIGHT WEEKS???*
- *OK, I have a copy, and I have my expired California license, perhaps that will work.*
- *I'll just put the car on cruise so that I don't get stopped.*
- *If I do I'll just explain . . . perhaps my British accent will help . . . Wait, I don't have my British license so that won't work.*

- *It will be fine, how often do I ever get stopped at home? Really, it should be fine.*
- *Hold on, every time I check in to a hotel I will get asked for identification, and I'll have to keep explaining. What if they don't accept my answer? What if they won't let me stay there? I'll have to find another hotel, they might all booked up, it might cost me more.*
- *Gosh I'm an idiot . . . so much for being organized . . .*

And on and on. I told Janice, and she looked at me and said, "But it's perfect, you have a photocopy of your license for exactly this eventuality. You couldn't have planned it better." She processed it for maybe a minute and she was done. About 30 minutes later, I started talking about it again, and she looked at me in amazement. "You're still worried about this? I'd forgotten about it already. It will be fine," she said.

> *"Freedom is a state of being unencumbered by limitations. Limitations of others and limitations we place upon ourselves. When we are truly free, we are shedding the doubt, restrictions, and boundaries we set on ourselves."*
>
> Christie, Maryland, USA

I was fascinated that Janice could process something like that so quickly. I decided to put it out of my mind, and it turned out to be astonishingly hard. I reflected on this as we were driving to Atlanta and came to the following conclusions:

- I felt like an idiot, and this is a place that I go to a lot. I got caught up in judgment of my own competence, wanting the trip to go perfectly, and I felt like I'd failed.
- I had a strong fear that other people would think I was an idiot and not like me. My self-judgment was driven by fear of losing connection to the people that are most important to me, and I go to this place a lot, too.
- I was worried that I would get in trouble if I were pulled over, because I'm fearful of breaking the rules.
- As I slowly came out of my negative spiral, I remembered my process for working through things. I have to talk things through to reach a new place. This allowed me to move out of a place of

9

judgment and show compassion for myself. It is a place that's challenging for me to get to. I have to work hard at it.

I wondered what would have happened if I hadn't been looking at life through the lens freedom this week? I think it would have taken me longer to accept that I am not perfect, realize that this was not the end of the world, and recognize that it was actually pretty amazing that I had planned a trip of this magnitude on my own. It was difficult, but I kept remembering one of the insights that Susan from Maryland had shared with me in response to my questions on freedom. Her story reminded me that I have a choice. I could react as I often do, by being hard on myself and heading down the negative spiral, or I could focus on responding differently. I could be mindful of my self-judgment, be kinder to myself, and trust there was something for me to learn from this situation, as Susan had related.

> *My dad was hiking. He came across a stream. In one direction the stream was all chaos with water crazily pouring over and down the rocks. Then he turned 180 degrees and saw at the other end of the stream was a calm pool of water into which the stream fed. He realized that no matter what is happening, there is almost always an alternative . . . sometimes you have to be open to seeing the difference 180 degrees away. To me this is true freedom . . . everything is a state of mind . . . and 180 degrees away might be the state of mind you need. Just open up your mind and give yourself the freedom to turn around 180 degrees.*

It wasn't easy, but by being mindful of freedom, consequences, and choices, I had a lens through which I could look at the situation differently. As the day wore on, I was less frustrated with myself. And when the consequence of my mistake turned out to be less than I'd feared, I was able to forgive myself for what I initially saw as stupidity. I started to accept myself for being human.

REFLECTION: What situations cause the monologue in your head to go down a negative spiral of self-judgment? Why is that? What do you notice about your reactions?

ACTION: Next time you find yourself going down that negative spiral, stop. What is the worst that could happen? What could you do differently? Try changing your reaction. How does that affect the outcome? What did you learn about yourself?

✍

"For to be free is not merely to cast off one's chains, but to live in a way that respects and enhances the freedom of others."[12] - Nelson Mandela

We explored the theme of Freedom while we traveled through the southeastern United States, where years ago many people did not have the luxury of freedom and choices. Without planning it, we came across historical places that threw a spotlight on the freedoms people have fought for, a spotlight on what happens when one group takes their own freedoms so far that there is a cost for others. We drove through Montgomery, Alabama, and visited the First White House of the Confederacy. The Selma-to-Montgomery March, a fifty-four-mile journey for voting rights, ended here in 1965 with Martin Luther King, Jr.'s speech on freedom. The March was about the freedom to choose who participates in a democracy. In New Orleans, we took a steamboat trip to Chalmette, where the Americans fought the British for independence. That battle was for Americans to have the freedom to make their own choices without having to answer to another country.

When we arrived in Chalmette, we took a tour. The Battle of Chalmette in 1815 was the last battle in the War of 1812, and we learned that many considered this to be the true War

> *"Freedom means 'choice' - choice to be who you are, or to discover who you are - to be true to yourself and to fulfill your potential, but in doing so, not impinge on/violate someone else's freedom".*
>
> *Jean, England*

of Independence, rather than the Revolutionary War of 1776. Josh was fascinated and asked a lot of questions. As the guide gave the statistics – 13 Americans killed, 2000 British killed – Josh exclaimed, "Wow, the Americans creamed the British!" The guide explained that the British had assumed the Americans wouldn't be well prepared. Josh replied, "Come on people, we're Americans, listen to us . . ." The guide and other tourists laughed. Freedom was so simple for a ten year old. Standing up to others who were restricting you seemed obvious to him; he couldn't imagine that anything would get in the way of his freedom.

> **REFLECTION**: Identify a situation in which you are truly constrained by someone else. What is standing in the way of claiming your freedom? Next, identify a situation where you are putting undue constraint on another. What is causing you to put this constraint in place?

> **ACTION**: Take action to stand up against those constraints. What happens? Now take action to remove the constraints you're putting on someone else. How does this impact your life? What do you learn about yourself?

As we came to the end of the first week, being mindful of freedom had given me the opportunity to think about life differently. I became more aware of the choices that I had and the consequences of those choices. I felt more carefree than I had in years. At the Riverwalk Marketplace in New Orleans, Josh held my hand as we walked toward a pole. He held on so tightly that we got trapped around it. He cracked up with laughter, walking into the pole over and over again, laughing harder each time. I looked at him in wonder, and laughed with him. It's so rare that I have time to fully enjoy and encourage his silliness, to not have to respond with, "Come on, we've got to be at (soccer, dinner, school . . . fill in the blank)." It felt like such a luxury to have the freedom to enjoy the moment.

> *"For me - freedom - is being outside, wind blowing in my hair, the scent of nature filling my soul - whether flowering trees, salt water, or the forest, sun beating on my face. It's a physical, very happy feeling - where nothing else matters but that moment."*
>
> *Heather, Massachusetts, USA*

Later that afternoon, on the boat back from Chalmette, I told Josh that we should do some research on the Civil War.

Karen: There's a lot of stuff about how that's related to our theme of freedom.

Josh: That's what makes America, America.

Karen: What's that?

Josh: Freedom. Even I know that and we haven't even done it at school yet!

As we took the streetcar back from Bourbon Street on our last night in New Orleans, I watched Josh talking to the driver, chatting away and laughing. I could feel the warm breeze from the open windows, and I felt truly relaxed. It was a beautiful, grounding feeling.

Complete the following sentences:

1. To me, freedom feels like ....

2. I feel most free when ....

3. I feel least free when ....

4. If I were to .... my sense of freedom would increase.

5. The implications of my most recent choices have been ....

Josh's Journal

Week 2

June 28th, 2012
My Mom had a big drama with her laptop, but we got it fixed.

June 29th, 2012
I went to Six Flags in San Antonio and went on five amazing roller coasters.

June 30th, 2012
We drove from San Antonio to Carlsbad. Bad.

July 1st, 2012
I went to Carlsbad Caverns. It had a lot of rock, and it was amazing.

July 2nd, 2012
I went to Santa Fe and it was different than Albuquerque.

July 3rd, 2012
Today I went on the second longest tramway in the world. It was awesome.

July 4th, 2012
Today I saw fireworks and went to an amusement park. Today was sizzling.

Impact

Week 2: Albuquerque, New Mexico; via San Antonio, Texas; and Carlsbad, New Mexico.

Total mileage so far: 3,323.

Theme for Week 2: Impact.

> **"A life is not important except in the impact it has on other lives."[13] - Jackie Robinson**

As I was deciding the theme for this week, I was reminded that "the last thing you learn about yourself is the impact you have on others" – a phrase from the instructor of a Dale Carnegie program I attended years ago in London. The truth of it has stayed with me, because thinking about and acknowledging the impact we have is often difficult. It's much easier to think about the impact others have on us, and focus on them, rather than take a look at ourselves. So I thought it would be interesting to hear people's perspectives and see the degree to which Josh could grapple with the concept.

A realization hit me when I was sitting at soccer practice one night, reading Brené Brown's new book, *Daring Greatly*.[14] Impact is all about how I show up. It is the attitude that I bring to a situation and how that affects the situation and others around me. It is also about what I observe and learn about my influence. It is noticing the impact others have on me, and then learning, through my reactions, about myself. And it is about what gets in the way of me showing up the way I intend to and achieving the outcome I want.

❧

"Everything you do has some effect, some impact."[15] - **Dalai Lama**

My first lesson in impact came when we arrived in San Antonio after a 550-mile drive from New Orleans. We checked into the hotel, and I turned on my laptop to find that the keyboard wouldn't work. I burst into tears, exhausted by the number of hours spent driving and overwhelmed by the thought of spending an unexpected $1,000. Josh looked very worried and asked what was wrong. I wailed, "My laptop's broken and I don't

> *"I think about impact in relation to the impact I have on others . . ."*
>
> Rachel, England

want to spend money on a new one right now." He started to get tearful, too. "It's OK, Mom," he said. "You can use the money from my account if you like." I could feel from the hug he gave me that I'd scared him, that he desperately wanted to help, and that he didn't want to me to be sad. I was overwhelmed by how much I loved this boy with such kindness in his heart.

I was, however, devastated by the impact I'd had on him. In my reaction to my broken laptop, I had shown vulnerability, and the effect on Josh had been striking. He wasn't used to seeing me this way. I'm uncomfortable showing vulnerability because it makes me feel weak, even though I know deep down that it requires strength. I want him to see me as strong and happy. In this case, I certainly hadn't intended to make him to feel so bad that he felt he had to contribute his own savings. I hugged him back, deciding not to gloss over it and pretend everything was fine. I wanted to show him that it's OK to be vulnerable, that it requires courage. By the strength of his hug, I realized that by showing my vulnerable side, I had increased the quality of my connection with him. I hugged him back with everything I had.

ACTION: Choose a situation in which you feel safe to show vulnerability and try demonstrating it.

REFLECTION: What is the impact on others? What happens to the quality of your connection with that person?

You may complete this exercise and all the exercises in the chapter in the exercise section at the back of the book and share your observations on my blog at: http://worklifeperspectives.com/Life_is_a_Road_Trip_.html

My laptop was still broken, so we decided to drive to Best Buy for help. In the car I started talking through my frustration out loud, saying things like, I never liked that laptop anyway, I knew I'd have to replace it at some point, maybe this was a sign that I need to purchase a Mac, etc. My external processing had an interesting effect on Josh.

> **Josh**: Mom, I think you should just stop, you're just making yourself more stressed.
>
> **Karen**: Oh no, I'm not actually. I have to talk about it so that I can think my way through something, and that helps me feel better about it. It actually makes me feel less stressed.
>
> **Josh:** Oh I never do that! I just end up feeling much worse.
>
> **Karen**: Was it making you feel stressed when I was talking about it?
>
> **Josh**: Yes.
>
> **Karen**: Oh I see. I'm sorry. So when you have a problem, or something bad happens, how do you work through it?
>
> **Josh**: Oh, I just think about it in my head. I tell myself I have to do better next time.
>
> **Karen**: Ah, that's interesting. Can you imagine that some people need to work through their problems differently than others?
>
> **Josh**: Yes, I guess so. I hadn't really thought of that before.
>
> **Karen**: Neither way is right or wrong, it's just different, and that's OK.

> *"Some people can leave you feeling energized and positive, others leave you feeling drained and negative."*
> *Fiona, England*

By being mindful of impact this week, I could see my method of problem solving was creating a problem for Josh. I remembered from the first week that I always have choices, so I decided to modify my behavior. When Josh said I was stressing myself out by processing out loud, it was really a reflection of the effect that I was having on him. It was a learning moment for both of us.

ACTION: The next time you are solving a problem, notice your approach and notice the impact on people around you.

REFLECTION: What do you see and hear? Was the impact positive or negative? What did you learn about yourself?

17

The next morning we took a trip to San Antonio's Six Flags Fiesta Texas amusement park. When you're ten (and arguably when you're forty-seven!) you can never visit too many amusement parks, and this was the first of many on our trip. On the way to the park, Josh left his sunglasses at a restaurant, and later he left his souvenir cup somewhere in the park. Without thinking about the possible impact, I said, "That's two things you've lost today." He was angry with himself and called himself stupid. I realized my comment had made him feel worse.

As I listened to him beating himself up, I realized a couple of things:

- My words could be considered a shaming comment, with the impact of making him feel stupid; they certainly didn't show empathy or understanding.
- Josh often calls himself an idiot when he makes a mistake. That's probably because I call myself an idiot at times, and he has learned it from me.

I heard my own reactions played back to me through him. I realized I haven't made clear to him that, as Brown says, "There

> *"The older I'm getting, the more I notice how much my words impact other people, so I am trying to be careful to never let myself be reckless with my words, even for a moment, since you can never really take something back after you say it."*
>
> *Stacy, Virginia, USA*

is a significant difference between you are bad and you did something bad."[16] We discussed this distinction on the way home from the park.

Josh: I'm such an idiot for losing two things. But I only lost thirty dollars worth of stuff and you lost one hundred and fifty dollars last night getting your laptop fixed.

Karen: You're not an idiot, you just did a silly thing. There's a difference between being a stupid person and making a mistake. It's not doing silly things that matters, it's how we handle them. And we both know that I don't do a very good job handling things based on how I reacted to my broken laptop last night!

Josh (laughing): That's right, you totally overreacted. I hate that about life, though – if only the bad things didn't happen!

Karen: I did overreact, and you helped me get a better perspective.

Josh: Yeah, I told you that you were just stressing yourself out even more . . . sheesh . . .

Karen: Well, perhaps we both should work on how we react to things to see if we can do a better job in future.

The lessons in this were rich for both of us. Even while being mindful of impact this week, it was still a challenge to see and anticipate the impact I was having at any point in time. But by paying attention, I noticed my impact more quickly than I might have otherwise.

REFLECTION: What tone do you use most often – encouraging, empathic, critiquing, shaming? Which approach makes you feel better and achieves the best result?

ACTION: The next time you make an observation to a co-worker, friend, or your children, think about the impact you want to have, and adjust your tone to line up with that. What was the result and what was the impact on them?

So how I show up – the sides of me that I choose to present at any given time – has the potential to impact people in many different ways. If I demonstrate vulnerability, it can increase connection with people I'm close to. The way I process situations can have a negative impact on others if their approach is different from mine. My tone of voice can unknowingly make someone feel bad even if that's not my intention. Rosalind from England shared the following story with me during the week, and it is a reminder that paying attention to our impact is difficult to remember, but rewarding.

A couple of months ago I attended a Regimental Dinner to mark the retirement of my first commanding officer. It was a glittering occasion, men in full mess kit, all scarlet and black and gold, ladies in evening dress, the tables laden with 200 years' accumulation of regimental silverware, including our beloved four-foot-high solid silver bear and our spectacular Fabergé pear blossom made of gold, crystal, jade and diamonds. In charge of the whole event was a portly little warrant officer (the highest rank you can reach in the British Army unless you apply for a commission). There was something familiar about his beaming smile, but I had no idea who he was. Afterwards he came straight over and announced that he owed his career to me – and it was then that I recognized him. Twenty-five years ago, when I last saw him, he was a skinny little recruit, always beaming, always getting into scrapes, and an absolute menace on the parade ground. I shall never forget the day when he turned to me and saluted – whilst holding a loaded sub-machine gun in his saluting hand . . . now that could have made an impact! For six months we nursed him through recruit training, and he made it in the end. Then I left and lost touch with the squadron, so I never knew how he got on as a soldier. Now I know the impact I had on him – and meeting him again made quite an impact on me too, all the more because I had absolutely no idea that I had played a small but significant part in what has turned out to be a very successful career.

☙

"The longer I live, the more convinced I become that life is 10 percent what happens to us and 90 percent how we respond to it." – Charles R. Swindoll[17]

Being mindful of impact this week also meant paying attention to the impact other people had on me. Taking that a step further, I decided to focus on what I learned from my reactions to others. It's relatively easy to notice the effect others have on us and blame them or look to them for explanations. It's much more difficult to examine how our own filters and biases affect our reactions. Doing so, though, is often revelatory.

There was an incident at Six Flags that raised my awareness of this. We were waiting in line for one of the rides, and a boy who was about six and his teen-age sister were in front of us. The boy asked his sister whether the ride would be scary, and she brushed off his concerns, telling him it wouldn't be scary at all and he would love it. He turned around to ask Josh and me whether it was scary. He looked terrified. I told him that we hadn't been on the ride yet, but that it had a rating of five, the highest for the thrill rides. I told him it was possible that it would be scary. It might still be fun, I told him, but there was definitely a chance it would be scary.

A few minutes later, his Mom joined the line. She told him that the ride would be fine, that he wouldn't be scared, and that he would love it. The situation bothered me immensely. I felt a visceral reaction, with the tension in my body rising with my building feelings of indignation. I wanted to intervene but felt it wasn't my place. So, rather than internally criticizing her parenting, I decided to reflect on what my reaction was telling me about myself. I realized what bothered me most was that this frightened boy's family wasn't listening to him. His feelings were not being validated. In fact, they were being brushed aside. From that, I recognized that being heard is really important to me, remembering the sting of not always feeling listened to in the past. I also concluded that I need to remember to listen closely to my son, my friends, and my colleagues in the future. I need to be more mindful of my impact and not brush people off with pat statements like, "It will be fine," or tell them, "Don't worry about it."

ACTION: The next time you feel yourself reacting to something someone says or does, pay close attention.

REFLECTION: What information does your reaction give you about yourself? What filters, biases, and lenses might be influencing your interpretation? How can you use this information to have a different impact in the future?

In the afternoon, I described my reaction to the incident to Josh. He said, "Perhaps they were just trying to cheer him up." Interesting. He had unknowingly pinpointed that I had allowed my own filters to get in the way of exploring what might have

> *"The impact someone can have on my life can be good or bad, and it can be intentional (they actually meant to have impact on me) or unintentional (they weren't trying to change my life, but something they did or said really affected me deeply for a long, long time, sometimes good and sometimes bad)."*
>
> *Stacy, Virginia, USA*

been going on for the mom and sister. I considered that one of the hardest things as a parent is seeing your child upset, scared, or unhappy. We want to protect our children and tell them it's going to be OK because we want it to be. The intentions of the mother and the sister were almost certainly good – they wanted him to have fun and be happy. There was just a misalignment of intent and impact.

ACTION: Take a piece of paper and pen and imagine your signature on that piece of paper. Look at the paper and think about it for at least a minute. Visualize the flow of your writing, how the letters come together effortlessly. Then using the opposite hand than you normally write with, write your signature on the paper.

REFLECTION: To what extent does the signature look anything like the visual you had in your mind? Where else in your life are your intentions good, but the delivery falls short? How can you modify that? How could that modification change the impact that you have and change how you show up?

Later that week we went to Cliff's Amusement Park in Albuquerque (see earlier comment that you can never visit too many amusement parks). We went on the bumper cars, which I don't enjoy at all. I don't like all the bumping, and I do my best to avoid the chaos by skirting around the outside. Josh loved it and went two or three more times on his own. As I watched, I wondered what this might be telling me about myself. My emotions didn't cause a physical response like in the earlier story, but I was irritated and frustrated that I couldn't control the bumping. I started to judge myself for thinking this way, when clearly bumper cars are all about bumping and chaos, but then I realized that this is who I am. I like creating order, I am not especially good with the unexpected, and I don't like chaos. I like it even less if I can't turn it into order.

Josh had a completely different reaction. He went in and out of the middle of the ring, bumping other cars with glee. He got stuck a few times, looked frustrated, got pushed to a better place by the attendant, and then carried on again. As I watched, it looked miserable to me, and I was convinced he would come off the ride feeling frustrated and annoyed. When bounced over to me, saying what great fun it was, I realized that my reaction had been all about me. I had projected onto him how I felt and assumed he would feel the same.

> **ACTION:** The next time you react to something notice what assumptions you are making, and what judgments you make.

> **REFLECTION:** Where do the judgments and assumptions come from? What does this tell you about the way that you interpret events in your life?

How I react to other people and situations gives me useful information about my motivations and what influences my reactions. Filters and biases also get in the way of empathy – in this situation, my ability to see how Josh was experiencing the bumper cars. I knew it would be interesting to explore empathy in a few weeks. With that deeper understanding, I increased my awareness of how I operate. Armed with this information, I could choose to approach situations differently in the future, instead of reacting without reflection or intention. When I show up thoughtfully and have a better insight into the impact I'm likely to have, I am more likely get a better outcome.

✐

"Don't let the noise of other people's opinions drown out your own inner voice."[18] - Steve Jobs

So what prevents us from having the impact we want to have? What makes us show up in overly cautious or other less than desirable ways? Often it is fear. We are afraid of displaying some kind of vulnerability, and we are afraid that we will not be accepted by others. Both affect our connection with those around us, and both influence the degree of belonging we feel in the world.

When we were at Cliff's Amusement Park, I went to purchase some drinks. The cashier told me I needed to purchase a "fun card" elsewhere in the park with my credit card, as the stand didn't take cash or credit cards. I sighed, exasperated that I had to go purchase a card and then line up again. I don't really know how my sigh and look of frustration made him feel. Perhaps, if he was self-confident enough, he thought I was the stupid one for not having read the signs; if he was more fragile, perhaps he felt stupid, even though it wasn't his fault.

I could have chosen a different response though. I could have thanked him for letting me know and apologized for not reading the signs. Instead, I allowed my own frustration to get in the way, and I moved quickly to a place of indignation. As Brown says, "When I am self righteous it means I'm afraid. It's a way to puff up and protect myself when I'm afraid of being wrong."[19]

My reaction was based on my own fear of looking stupid or incompetent. It was easier to pass this feeling on to him than it was to pause, notice what was going on, and allow myself to feel vulnerable. If I hadn't been paying attention to impact this week, I might have lost a vital piece of information about myself. I might not have understood the degree to which fear of looking stupid gets in the way of having a positive impact or responding to people with kindness. I wish I had gone back to the young man and apologized for my rudeness. I imagine that both of us would have felt better. Josh would have learned the valuable message that even though we aren't perfect, there is always an opportunity to recover and attempt to make something right.

REFLECTION: What characteristic of yourself are you most afraid of people seeing? To what lengths do you go to in order to hide that from the world?

ACTION: Next time you feel are feeling vulnerable because of this, choose a different behavior. How does it feel? What was the result?

Later that week we went to the pool, and there was a boy swimming who was about Josh's age. Josh spent about an hour shuffling around the edge of the pool in the water. When I suggested he go and play with the other boy, Josh made every excuse not to talk to him – he's busy, he's with his family, he might not want me to, etc. The next day at lunch, I asked him about it.

Karen: I have a question. Did you not talk to that boy at the pool yesterday because you felt uncomfortable starting the conversation?
Josh: Yes! That's right!

Karen: I don't like starting conversations with people I don't know either. And then someone told me once that a lot of people don't like it, so they're relieved if someone else does, and often grateful.
Josh: Hmmmm . . .

"There's something sacred that happens between a parent and a child when the parent says, 'Me too!'," Brené Brown says.[20] Even at a young age, the fear of what other people will think of us is powerful. It was clear to me that Josh was dying to spend time with other kids, but that he was struggling with how to engage.

Josh: Sometimes I suck at . . . being myself.
Karen: Oh Josh, what makes you say that?
Josh: I really want to be cool, and then I'm not myself.
Karen: Ah . . . do you worry about what people will think about you?
Josh: Yes!!
Karen: Me, too. That's hard isn't it?
Josh: Yes, I act in a certain way so that they won't think I'm stupid.

That evening we went to the Fourth of July celebrations at the Balloon Museum in Albuquerque. There were a number of activities and many children around Josh's age. It didn't take him long to find someone to play with on the moon bounces and to join in a game of volleyball. The look of joy on his face from being part of the group, from the sense of acceptance, was incredible to see. I was so proud of him for overcoming his fears. I am not sure how much our prior conversations impacted him, or what gave him the courage to engage, but it was clear from the look on his face that his sense of connection to the world was enhanced. He had learned, in this moment, to show up differently.

ACTION: Identify a situation or future event where you are worried that you will not be accepted by the group. Carefully plan a strategy for engaging, and think about how you want to impact other people.

REFLECTION: How did it feel to go through this process? What result did you want, and what result did you get?

So, impact is about how I show up, about the influence that I have on people and situations. During this week I was able to observe the impact I had on other people, and I learned that making myself vulnerable can increase the quality of my connection with others. I observed my reactions to the impact of others on me, and I learned to use that information to understand myself better. I observed what got in the way of making the impact I want, and I learned that the fear of not being accepted can result in a more cautious or less positive way of engaging in life. The more we learn about and accept ourselves for who we are, the less power fear has over us. We know we're OK, we know we're enough, and we can have the impact that we want.

As we were leaving New Mexico, I asked Josh about his final thoughts on Impact. He replied that he really didn't have any more thoughts, except that he thought the topic of freedom was easier. I asked him whether he had any more thoughts on the impact he has on other people. He replied, "I don't know, because I'm not them." I knew empathy would be interesting to explore later in the trip. As we drove through the great expanse of barren countryside in New Mexico, I saw a billboard that said simply, "Smile at someone." It actually did make me smile, so I turned to Josh and gave him a really big smile. He smiled back, and we both laughed softly. Sometimes, all it takes to have a positive impact is a smile.

Complete the following sentences:

1. The impact that I want to have on others is ....
   because..........................

2. I will know that I have had that impact when I see...........................
   and feel ....

3. When I am.......................it's hard to have the impact that I want

4. To me, vulnerability feels ....

5. I resist feeling vulnerable in the following situations
   ....

Josh's Journal

Week 3

July 5th, 2012
Today we drove from Albuquerque to the Grand Canyon. Today was not the best.

July 6th, 2012
Today was amazing. I saw and hiked the Grand Canyon. The best day yet.

July 7th, 2012
Today was good. I saw a tour of the d-backs stadium and an amazing game of the Arizona Diamondbacks. Today was great.

July 8th, 2012
Today I went to Joshua Tree National Park and saw *Spiderman*. Second best day.

July 9th, 2012
Today I went to a beach in San Diego. Amazing.

July 10th, 2012
Today I went to the San Diego Zoo Safari Park and saw a cheetah run up close. Beast.

July 11th, 2012
Today I went to Disney California Adventure. I went and saw a lot of cool stuff. Nice Day.

July 12th, 2012
Today I went to Universal Studios and went on a roller coaster, 2 4-D things and a simulator ride. Sweet Day.

Kindness

Week 3: Anaheim, California, via Williams, Arizona (Grand Canyon); Phoenix, Arizona; Yucca Valley and San Diego, California.

Total mileage so far: 4,337.

Theme for Week 3: Kindness.

> **"Three things in human life are important; the first is to be kind. The second is to be kind. The third is to be kind."[21] – Henry James**

As I sat down to write this chapter, I noticed it was November 13, World Kindness Day. The World Kindness Movement started World Kindness Day in 1998, and it's observed in many countries including Canada, the United Kingdom, Japan, Australia, Nigeria and United Arab Emirates. The purpose is to encourage people to look beyond the boundaries of their culture, race, and country, and focus on what we have in common, rather than our differences.

I smiled at the coincidence. When you start to pay attention to something, it seems to keep showing up. In the third week of our trip, I really started to see the relationship between our weekly themes. There is a clear and strong connection between impact and kindness. As I started to practice kindness during the third week, I could feel that I appeared more positive to those around me. The impact of that positivity led to more kindness. But I also saw that my fear of looking stupid in front of others consistently gets in the

> *"Kindness is simple, costs nothing but can have a huge impact."*
>
> *Rachel, England*

way of my showing up the way I want to show up. This was my Achilles' heel, and it had the potential to undermine my ability to be kind. As I reflected on this during the trip and became more mindful of it, I was able to come to terms with it. My level of self-acceptance increased.

29

Josh has a book called *How Full Is Your Bucket? For Kids.* It uses the metaphor of buckets and dippers to show the impact of positive and negative moments in life. As positive things happen, your bucket becomes fuller; as negative things happen, the bucket dips and empties. The fullness of your bucket affects everyone around you, the quality of your relationships and your connection with life.[22] There were many moments this week when my bucket was full and others when my own actions emptied it.

It's easy to get sidetracked by the minutiae of our days and by our inability to be compassionate toward ourselves and toward others. Practicing kindness takes intention and focus. And that intention has to come from a positive place. Otherwise the impact of our actions drains our buckets a little, and the buckets of those around us. We all have an opportunity to habituate kindness and make it a more regular part of what we bring to the world. Perhaps if we practiced kindness more often, we wouldn't need World Kindness Day.

⟳

"Practice random acts of kindness and senseless acts of beauty."[23] - Anne Herbert

When we arrived at our motel near the Grand Canyon, we found a package my neighbor Meg had sent containing my driver's license, which I had discovered I had forgotten early in the trip. This was the first act of kindness for the week. Without a doubt, Meg had showed incredible kindness. She had listened to me stress about where I should have her send it. She had gone to the post office and then to FedEx because the post office wouldn't guarantee next day delivery. She had scanned and e-mailed the receipt to reassure me. She didn't have to do any of that. She did it all out of the kindness of her heart, and I felt grateful. The start of the third week felt good, and my bucket became a little fuller.

The next morning we planned to take a train to the Grand Canyon, and I got up early to get the tickets printed. The receptionist at the hotel front desk told me the printer was broken. I looked at him in alarm. I don't usually leave things to the last minute, and I worried we wouldn't be able to get on the train. He

> *"One small act of kindness can give someone hope and make them feel loved".*
> *Stacy, Virginia, USA*

suggested other places I could have the tickets printed, but none of them were open. I started to think I was never going to get the tickets.

I panicked, telling the receptionist again that the train was leaving in two hours, as if that explanation would magically fix the printer. Luckily the receptionist was both patient and kind. He didn't have to keep trying to fix the machine, but he did. It started to feel like we were a team coming up with different options for printing the tickets. I went out into the lobby in exasperation while he tried to solve the problem one more time, and suddenly I heard a shriek of joy. He'd found the problem: a toothbrush jammed in the printer (really!). We laughed together. I printed the tickets, and we were good to go.

Was he obligated to try so hard to fix the printer and get me my tickets? Not really. I wasn't staying at an expensive hotel with a business center where that service might have been expected. He went above and beyond in trying to solve my problem for me. I have no doubt that it was, in part, because he was a kind person. Being mindful of kindness this week allowed me to see his actions as kind and helped me avoid getting overly stressed or having unrealistic expectations about his obligation to print my tickets. It helped me manage my frustration with the situation and myself. I also believe that treating him kindly and respectfully helped us make a connection through trying to solve a problem. And I believe both of us had fuller buckets at the end of the experience.

> **ACTION:** For the rest of the day, approach every interaction that you have with kindness.

> **REFLECTION:** What happens to the quality of your connection with the people that you interact with? How does it make you feel to approach life with kindness?

You may complete this exercise and all the exercises in the chapter in the exercise section at the back of the book and share your observations on my blog at: http://worklifeperspectives.com/Life_is_a_Road_Trip_.html

Later that week we took a tour of Chase Field in Phoenix, home of the Diamondbacks baseball team. The Diamondbacks were playing that evening, and we decided to stay for a game. Josh loves baseball games; I love watching the excitement and enthusiasm on his face. During the game, Josh turned into an ardent Diamondbacks fan. I was just happy the stadium was air conditioned to a balmy seventy-nine degrees. Josh's enthusiasm infected everyone around him, and at one point someone in the row in front of us offered him a box of popcorn. He was surprised, didn't quite know how to respond, and declined. I told the woman that she was kind to offer, and she offered again. Perhaps she was grateful that Josh was such an enthusiastic fan, or perhaps his positive energy was contagious. But more likely she was simply kind.

We noticed two other stories during the week about random acts of kindness. The first was in Anaheim. Instead of a panhandler we all often see, there was a man standing on a street corner giving away five dollar bills. He held a sign that read, "Have car and home." A local TV station reported that he had decided to give money away as a random act of kindness to celebrate his birthday. He made an intentional choice to practice kindness. People were overjoyed, even though he was stopping the traffic and causing chaos in an already congested part of Southern California. The story of this unexpected random act of kindness warmed my heart. I suspect his bucket, and the buckets of everyone he touched with his kindness that day, were fuller.

The second random act of kindness also took place in Anaheim, as we were walking around Universal Studios. Typically, there is very little to observe in the way of kindness at amusement parks. People seem at their worst, pushing to the front of the line in restaurants, hopping in and out of line at the rides. As we lined up for The Simpsons Ride, immediately I could see people scoping out the entrance to the ride. Each car had two rows of seats with four seats in each row. Because of the way the numbers worked out, someone in the group ahead of us was going to be separated from friends or family. I found myself in an internal dialogue, thinking:

- Should I be the one to offer to split up, because I can see that the older woman wants to stay with her party?
- But I'm a single mom, and I want to be with my son.
- But it would be an act of kindness, I can see that this woman looks frightened to ride without her group.

> "I think acts of kindness are things that not only put others before yourself but that they are things that are considerate of the other people's feelings."
>
> Liz, England

Then one of the people waiting offered to sit separately from his group so that she could stay with her family. It was surprising to see someone act out of kindness, in an environment that can exhibit rudeness and American commercialism at its worst. I wished I had stepped forward. After all, Josh enjoys doing things on his own, so he would have been fine. I missed an opportunity to make my bucket fuller. I was grateful to see, though, that someone else took the opportunity to fill the nervous lady's bucket as she stepped on to the ride.

ACTION: Pick a moment to bestow a random act of kindness on someone you don't know.

REFLECTION: What was their reaction? How did that make you feel? What do you think the impact was on the person to whom you showed kindness?

⤜⤏

"Kindness gives birth to kindness."[24] – Sophocles

Not only do random acts of kindness have a positive impact on people's well being, they often lead to other acts of kindness. In his book *The Hidden Power of Kindness*, Lawrence G. Lovasik says, "No kind action ever stops with itself. One kind action leads to another."[25]

At the Diamondbacks game, we ordered dinner at a fast food counter. Josh asked for a burrito without onions or sour cream – just beans, chicken and cheese. The cashier seemed surprised; this was not the kind of place where they made food to order. Flustered, she entered the meal into the cash register for one dollar more than it should have been. She had to get her supervisor, who told us we would have to wait until she could open the cash register to give us credit. The cashier looked rattled and embarrassed. Sympathizing with her, I told her not to worry, that it wasn't a problem. She started to explain that the register keys are close

> *"Kindness . . . is what we should all practice daily. It is a good healer for our lives, as you give kindness your heart will fill with peace and more kindness will be returned to you in many different forms."*
>
> *Antonio, California, USA*

together, that she made a mistake, and that it was an accident. I tried to reassure her again that it really was not a problem. She looked relieved and grateful, and before I could turn around, she handed Josh a free churro.

As I walked away, I realized that when I am kind, people around me not only feel better, but they become kinder, too. I could have become frustrated with the cashier for making a mistake and holding us up when we were anxious to get back to the game. But being mindful of kindness gave me pause, and I chose a different response. That mindfulness allowed me to see that there is a domino effect when I am kind. It gave me an opportunity to see the connection between my attitude and the effect it has on everyone around me. I realized that kindness is about paying it forward. As Aesop wrote centuries ago, "No act of kindness, no matter how small, is wasted."[26]

REFLECTION: Reflect on the opportunities you have to be intentionally kind in a situation where you otherwise might not, such as a work situation where your colleagues expect you to behave in a certain way, the chaos of a crowded mall, or an encounter with an estranged friend or family member. Choose an opportunity where you know the other person will not be expecting kindness.

ACTION: Deliberately show up differently. Smile when you might have frowned; say thank you when you might not typically remember. Show kindness with intention. What happens?

∽

"There is no choice between being kind to others and being kind to ourselves. It is the same thing."[27] **– Piero Ferucci**

There was always something that got in the way of our themes, just as there is always something

> *"I think kindness to oneself in some of it's best form is self-acceptance and unconditional self love . . . something most of us do very poorly for ourselves."*
>
> *Susan, Maryland, USA*

that stops us having the impact that we want. Kindness was no exception. When we were in Phoenix, we went to get breakfast from the hotel buffet and we brought it back to the room so we could watch the men's final of Wimbledon on TV as we ate. As we approached the door, I dropped my oatmeal on the floor and got incredibly irritated with myself. I'd stacked too many things in my arms, thinking it would be more efficient to carry everything in one trip. As I looked at the mess on the floor, I called myself stupid, huffed a lot, and cursed under my breath. Josh tried to help me, but I got irritated with him too. In reality, though, I was only irritated with myself. My Achilles' heel — my vulnerability about looking incompetent or doing something stupid — was back. I started judging myself, and that prevented me from showing kindness to either Josh or myself.

Later that day, as we were driving to Joshua Tree National Park, CA, Josh and I discussed kindness.

Karen: So Josh, what do you think kindness is?
Josh: I don't know.
Karen: Well, who or what do you think has shown kindness to you?
Josh: Well you saved up and paid for this trip – that was kind.
Karen: Oh, you're welcome. What about when you do something kind for other people?
Josh: Well, I tried to help you clean up this morning, but I got yelled at.
Karen: Oh I'm so sorry. You're right. I guess I didn't have my kindness on yet this morning, did I?
Josh (laughing): No you didn't!

I felt terrible. I told him that I was annoyed with myself and that was why I reacted the way I did. He said, "Yes, and you took it out on me." I felt even worse. My judgment of myself and the lack of compassion I showed myself in that moment had a direct impact on my son. My bucket was drained, and I knew that I had drained his bucket too. Judgment of, and an inability to be compassionate toward, ourselves gets in the way of showing kindness. If we find it hard to show kindness to ourselves, we will find it hard to show and see kindness in others. Showing myself kindness is obviously something that doesn't come naturally.

As I reflected on this, I realized something else. It wasn't just my lack of compassion for myself that blocked my ability to give and receive kindness. It was that my self-judgment was tied to how well I accept myself. If I could accept that I am human and make mistakes, it would be easier to show myself compassion in those frustrating moments that everyone has. If I can learn to do that for myself, I can learn to do it with others. In her book *The Force of Kindness,* Sharon Salzburg writes that kindness "helps us to genuinely care for one another and for ourselves as well."[28]

> **REFLECTION**: What is your Achilles' heel when it comes to your ability to show kindness to yourself? What triggers this? What happens when it shows up?

> **ACTION**: The next time you feel your Achilles' heel showing up, stop. Change your actions and choose to be more kind to yourself. What is the impact on yourself and those around you?

Later in the week, I noticed again how challenging I find being kind to myself, even when I'm paying attention. We were in San Diego, I was tired, and it felt like everything kept going wrong. The Wi-Fi in the hotel didn't work, the toilet was blocked, and the TV had no sound. Then I kept dropping everything: my clothes as I took them out of my case, my phone every time I picked it up, my shampoo and conditioner as I carried them to the bathroom. I was really trying not to let my frustration and exhaustion show and trying not to distress Josh the way I had in Phoenix. Despite my focus, it was

> *"I sure hope that you are being kind to yourself, and not driving too hard in pursuit of enlightenment . . . be sure to stop and smell the (Albuquerque) roses!"*
> *Walter, California, USA*

challenging. Then I paused for a moment. Couldn't I be a bit kinder to myself? I'd driven more than 4,000 miles in three weeks, we had stopped for no more than a couple of nights at a time, and many of our activities required organizing. My mental and physical exhaustion was completely reasonable. Why was it so hard to show myself some understanding?

Just thinking about it helped for a while, until we went to play mini golf before our trip to the Safari Park. The course was closed, even though according to the website it should have been open. We went to Starbucks to kill some time instead. But I beat myself up for not calling to confirm the opening time.

Josh: Mom, I think you should calm down. You're sounding stressed.

Karen: That's not helping!!!

Josh: OK . . . ...

Karen: Sorry, this is not your fault. I'm feeling tired and frustrated and very irritable as a result.

Josh: That's OK, I know you got that from Nana and Granddad.

I laughed out loud, and Josh's ability to make me laugh made me feel lighter. I told him that I hope he doesn't learn to respond to situations with irritation like I do. But as I was saying it, I realized that he already did respond to some situations with the same frustration and irritation. I vowed to be kinder to myself, knowing I need to model the behavior I want him to learn.

ACTION: Spend the next week being deliberately kind to yourself.

REFLECTION: How hard was it? How often did you have to remind yourself to be kind? What was the impact when you remembered to be kind to yourself?

Even when you're mindful, it is difficult to change habits that have developed over a lifetime. I have heard that to create a new behavior you have to do it twenty-one times in a row. Growing up, I wasn't told that I should be kind to myself or

"Kindness . . . an underestimated characteristic."

Orla, Northern Ireland

taught that it was something to be valued. So, like most things, being kind to myself is something that requires practice, especially if bad habits typically interfere. If it is difficult to be kind to yourself, then it's difficult to be kind to others. Conversely, when we are kinder to ourselves, it's easier to be kinder to others. "Kindness is compassion in action," Salzburg says.[29] Showing ourselves compassion allows us to accept who we are, mistakes and all.

"Kindness is a language that the deaf can hear and the blind can see."[30] **– Mark Twain**

In Arizona, after we took the train to the Grand Canyon, we decided to hike down the canyon. Josh was so excited that he wanted to go all the way to the bottom. But it was too far for one day – we would have needed to camp and we were not equipped to do so. Besides, I don't like camping! Then, in his enthusiasm, Josh tripped, fell, and caught his knee on a rock. It started to bleed a little. Someone stopped and told me that Josh's cut needed water, that I should wash it immediately. He started squirting water on the wound. He took over, treating me as if I were barely even present. After recovering from my shock at his brashness, I reasserted myself, thanking him and telling him we were fine.

My reaction was one of indignation, and it took me a while to figure out why. After all, he didn't have to stop and help, so why did it not feel kind? I

"I think kindness comes from the heart and it's to do with the spirit in how you treat other people- you can you can go to great ends to help people or be generous but if it's not done in the right spirit it feels horrible to the receiver."

Fiona, England

recalled a phrase I often use when I am running workshops: Assume noble intent. So if I assumed that he meant to be helpful and didn't intend to be condescending and patronizing, why did it leave me cold? I realized that it wasn't his actions, but his delivery.

As Ferrucci says, "Someone who tries to show how clever [he] is cannot be truly kind. [His] kindness will be condescending."[31] It felt as if the passer by assumed that I could not manage without help, and he needed to show me he knew better. If he'd asked me what I needed, or offered up his help in a supportive, caring, or concerned way, then his message would have been dramatically different. But he didn't. And so the potential for kindness was lost.

Later that day, on the train back to Williams, the host of our train car regaled us with fascinating stories of living in the desert, building her own home, and living "off the grid" forty-five miles from the nearest grocery store and eighty-three miles from the nearest hardware store. Through her stories, her love for the beauty of the Grand Canyon was clear. She passed through the train car, stopping to talk to each family and offering tips on places to visit, stay, and hike. She did so in a kind way, she listened to what each family had to say, and she shared her story. The feeling from her kind gestures was entirely different than the hiking experience. I believe the man who helped Josh intended to be kind. But it was much easier to receive the kindness of the hostess.

ACTION: The next time you have an opportunity to show someone kindness, pay close attention to how you deliver this kindness.

REFLECTION: How did you show up? Were you supportive, did you listen, were you empathetic? How do you think paying attention to your delivery affected the other person?

As we pulled into Williams, the hostess thanked us for listening and said, "There is so much to learn from each other in our stories." As I looked back on our stories from this week, I saw again the opportunity that presents itself when we are mindful. We have the opportunity to improve our awareness and understanding of ourselves and our motivations. We learn that we have choices and that when we act with intention we can have the impact that we want. Salzburg says, "To commit to living with kindness we need to develop mindfulness as well. As we grow increasingly aware of what we are thinking and feeling just when it is occurring, we see how that allows us to make a conscious choice to act in accord with our deeply held values."[32]

And so, without planning it, our weekly themes started to weave together. Freedom allowed us the space to be ourselves, to try different approaches, to make choices. Impact explored our attitudes, the effect we have on others, and what we learn about ourselves by considering the impact others have on us. Practicing kindness had an uplifting effect on others and contributed to us being present in a more positive way. It also had a domino effect because our kindness to one person often leads them to be kind to others. Finally, as Salzburg says, "The practices of kindness inspire and deepen our connection to ourselves and one another."[33] As we began the fourth week, where our theme would be connection, Salzburg's words indicated another link. "Kindness points to the core of what it means to be alive, which is to be connected."

Complete the following sentences:

1. When I am kind to others ....

2. When I am kind to myself ....

3. It is hard to be kind to others when ....

4. It is hard to be kind to myself when ....

5. Kindness is related to connection because ....

Josh's Journal

Week 4

July 13th, 2012
Today my Mom bought a Mac Book Pro, so I'll get my Mom's Toshiba.

July 14th, 2012
Today I went and saw elephant seals and Hearst Castle.

July 15th, 2012
Today my Mom drove to Yosemite, and when we got there we chillaxed.

July 16th, 2012
Today I hiked 5.4 miles in Yosemite. Nice.

July 17th, 2012
Today we drove to a friend's house and chilled. OK day.

July 18th, 2012
Today I went to Six Flags and did a lot of roller coasters. Very cool!

July 19th, 2012
Today I went to the pool. Then got pizza. OK.

July 20th, 2012
I saw my old houses in San Francisco. Sad.

Connection

Week 4: Bay Area, California; via Paso Robles and Yosemite, California.

Total mileage so far: 5,018.

Theme for Week 4: Connection.

"No man is an island, entire of itself."[34] **- John Donne**

In the third week, the relationship between kindness and connection started to emerge. When kindness is practiced, a connection is created and strengthened. However, when Josh and I talked about connection, our theme for the fourth week, he had an entirely different perspective.

> **Karen**: So our theme this week is connection – what do you think that means?
> **Josh**: Electronics.
> **Karen**: What do you mean by that?
> **Josh**: Poles, wires and so on so that people can text each other.

For me, this week was about reconnecting with old friends. It was about exploring whether you need to be with someone in person to remain connected, or whether a connection can survive physical absence. It was about how memories influence connection and about staying connected during difficult conversations. And, as always, it was about what gets in the way – our

> *"There are almost too many possibilities – 'being connected' – being close to someone – sharing thoughts, ideas, a way of life. Staying connected – keeping in touch – 'a sense of connection' could be with like-minded people family, friends, a group of people who share similar aims, values, interests . . . "*
>
> *Jean, England*

inability to stay present in the moment, our need for approval, and our judgments of ourselves.

When we arrived in the San Francisco Bay Area, my friend Ann shared the following metaphor about connection she adapted from imagery her brother used to share when he taught at a Catholic school.

> *Connection is a blanket woven of love from two different threads. As the blanket is created, its color, texture and pattern change based on what materials are used. Two different threads uniquely woven can create an entire blanket. If there is love, respect and kindness, the blanket will last. It will be elastic when pulled or pinched. It will give when strained.*
>
> *If there is no love, when pulled, the material will rip. Like a tear in any garment, the hole can get larger if it is not patched. The material or connection can fall apart. Each blanket and connection is unique because we each contribute a unique part of ourselves to be shared with another unique self. It has never existed before in time and will never have the opportunity to exist in this time again.*

If we show love, kindness, and respect to ourselves and to others, we can strengthen our connections. We bring our unique contributions to the world and weave connections based on our similarities, along with curiosity about our differences. If we get caught up in judgments and fail to show kindness, empathy, and understanding, the fabric of our connections becomes strained. If we don't work to fix them, those connections may be permanently broken. Through connection we find belonging. Through connection we are part of something, and we are not alone in the world.

෴

"A good friend is a connection to life – a tie to the past, a road to the future, the key to sanity in a totally insane world."[35] - Lois Wyse

I opened Facebook as we prepared to drive to Paso Robles, California, and a friend had posted the following:

*It's been said that everlasting friends go long periods of time
without ever speaking, and never question their friendship.
These friends pick up phones like they just spoke yesterday,
regardless of how long it has been or how far away they
live, and they don't hold grudges. They understand that life
is busy and that you will always love them. Share if you have
at least 1 of these friends – they will know who they are.*

The next few weeks would be filled with visits to people who would
have known I was talking about them when I shared this post. I'd spoken
to some of the friends we were visiting on the West Coast regularly during
the eight years since I left California, others hardly at all. My connections
felt faded when I didn't see them, but they were still there in the
background. When we were together, the connections revived and
became brighter.

My friend Ann and
I had both worked hard
to retain our connection
through phone calls and

> *"With a friend, it always feels good when together,
> and distance makes no difference."*
> Orla, Northern Ireland

e-mails. Distance had been no object. While we chatted in the sun in her
backyard, watching Josh and her sons playing, we nourished our connection
more. The blanket of our connection still existed, but as we sat together the
weave tightened and the colors became more vibrant. Being together was
important, but not vital, for the connection to remain. It is our common
interests, and the curiosity and respect we have for our differences, that
prevents the blanket from tearing.

Later, after Josh had called one of his buddies in Maryland, I realized
that for him, connection was all about being with someone in person.

Karen: So was it nice reconnecting with Tim yesterday?
Josh: What do you mean? I didn't connect with him.
Karen: You called him and talked
to him on the phone.
Josh: That's not connecting – you
have to see someone to connect
with them.

> *"I think we feel most connection with
> another person when we are with them
> in person."*
> Fiona, England

Karen: Oh, really?
Josh: Yes, duh, aren't you the life coach?

Despite this, he intuitively knew that to maintain a connection you have to work at it. He missed his friend Tim while we were on our trip, talked about him all the time, and sent him many text messages. For Josh, electronics offered a way to maintain a friendship, but they were no substitute for being together. Still, when we got back home, their connection was stronger than ever.

ACTION: Reread the Facebook post from above and notice who springs to mind. Pick up the phone, or write an e-mail to contact them. If they live locally, visit them.

REFLECTION: What happens to the nature of your connection? How does it change based on whether you talk via e-mail, phone or in person? What could you do to enhance the connection?

You may complete this exercise and all the exercises in the chapter in the exercise section at the back of the book and share your observations on my blog at: http://worklifeperspectives.com/Life_is_a_Road_Trip_.html

❧

"As long as the memory of certain beloved friends lives in my heart, I shall say that life is good."[36] **- Helen Keller**

While we were in California, the relationship between memories and connection became apparent. We stayed in Paso Robles with Alan, the widower of a great friend of mine who died suddenly a couple of years ago. Toby had been one of my favorite people, and I had come to know her husband well because of my friendship with her. During the visit I slept in her office, with everything apparently

> *"I can sometimes have a very strong connection to a song because the lyrics are very specific for me or because the melody is just so beautiful."*
> *Stacy, Virginia, USA*

still in the place it was before she died. As I walked in, I could feel her presence everywhere. My head and heart filled with memories of her – hikes we went on, conversations we had, our laughter during Thanksgiving dinners with her family. As Alan and I talked, I felt connected to her again, because the memories were so powerful.

Music can also spark memories. As we drove toward the Bay Area, we listened to a Natalie Merchant album that I used to play when I first moved to San Francisco. One song in particular, "San Andreas Fault," reminded me of the beauty of California, the opportunity there, and the irony of its propensity for devastating natural disasters. The music triggered a strong feeling of connection to the place and to that period of my life. I felt like I had sixteen years before, with all the excitement that living in California had brought.

Later that week, Ann and I took the train to San Francisco to meet some friends at Palomino, one of my favorite restaurants along The Embarcadero. I had invited everyone I knew in the Bay Area to come for drinks. As I looked up at the Bay Bridge, with the lights shining, I had an overwhelming sense of belonging. I didn't live here anymore, but an important part of my life journey had been spent here. I was reminded how lucky I had been to live in this beautiful city. I felt fortunate to be able to revive the connection with these friends who were so important during that time in my life. The weave in my blanket of connection to this place and these people was strengthened, and perhaps so was my connection to myself.

ACTION: Search for a memory of a place, a person, or an event. Think about it for a while and relive it.

REFLECTION: How does it feel? To what degree do you feel reconnected with that part of your life? How does that make you feel about yourself? What did you learn from reliving that memory?

At the end of the week, Josh and I drove around San Francisco. We visited our old houses. I pointed out our favorite places and houses where our friends used to live. We went roller blading along The Embarcadero, which had been a regular Sunday morning activity for me before Josh

> *"The opposite to being connected is being isolated, which is one of the most awful things you can do to a person."*
> *Fiona, England*

was born. But I was surprised by how uninterested Josh was by this trip down memory lane. He grunted at our old houses and sighed whenever I exclaimed, "Oh look - that's the [fill in the blank], we used to go there a lot!" To my surprise, he resisted roller blading, although he had loved it when we skated along the boardwalk in San Diego.

And then it struck me. There was no connection here for him. He was two years old when we left San Francisco. It was hard for him to be enthusiastic about things he didn't remember. And worse, he felt left out, because I was so obviously excited by being here, and he wasn't. He felt disconnected and isolated from the memories that were providing me with connection. We packed up our roller blades, got back in the car, and went to meet friends for lunch. I had fed my need for connection; I didn't want my connection with Josh to become strained because he felt excluded. I wanted us to create new memories that would become a connection for him. I wanted him to create his own feeling of belonging, a foundation from which he could grow.

REFLECTION: Think of a time when you unintentionally made someone feel isolated. What was the circumstance? How quickly did you notice something was wrong? What was the impact on your connection with them? What might help you to recognize such a situation in the future and how could you moderate your approach?

ACTION: Put your new approach into practice. What happens to your connection now?

☙

"How relationships unfold with the most important people in our lives depends on courage and clarity in finding voice."[37] - Harriet Lerner

As we were traveling this week, I was also focused on an issue that had been brewing for months and that had the potential to strain my connection with Josh. At Christmastime, we had gone dog sledding, and Josh had looked so happy hugging the dogs after the ride. Over dinner that night, he had asked whether we could have a dog, and I hadn't said "no." Instead, I said something like, "Maybe when you're in middle school."

But that answer put me in a tough spot. I don't like dogs. And as a single parent, managing the logistics of life, full-time work, and sports activities for Josh was already challenging. The thought of having a dog, with all the additional work involved, was beyond daunting. As I fretted, Josh started talking more regularly about what kind of dog we'd have, the schedule for walking and feeding, and how we could bring the dog with us to soccer games. My anxiety level increased, and I woke up in a cold sweat a couple

> *"You don't really build a connection with someone by just talking about simple things like the weather!"*
>
> Stacy, Virginia, USA

of nights, knowing that I should have done a better job of managing this conversation. As we drove, the issue loomed; it was a difficult conversation that I needed to have.

So how do you have a difficult conversation and remain connected with someone? I didn't want to ruin our great vacation by telling Josh we couldn't have a dog, but I didn't want to get one either. If I hadn't been paying attention to connection this week, I might have become irritated every time we discussed it. I'd have used every possible opportunity to explain why we shouldn't have a dog, including pointing out things we wouldn't be able to do anymore if we had a dog, possibly using a tone that suggested Josh was silly for even thinking it was possible. Actually, I started down this path a few times, and then caught myself. At the end of the fourth week, we had lunch with my former boss Robert and learned that his wife, Sandy, volunteers in a dog shelter. Josh started asking questions, told her that we would have a dog one day, and described what he thought it would be like. She kindly explained to Josh how having a dog changes your life and how important it is to take that kind of responsibility seriously. His enthusiasm dampened a bit, but not enough to give up the idea.

In her book *The Dance of Connection*, Harriet Lerner explains, "It is possible to speak honestly and also to proceed with care to protect a relationship that is important to us."[38] Could I find the courage to have that difficult conversation about the dog, and would I have the skill to stay connected at the same time? Could I stay true to my message and yet deliver it with kindness? My anxiety and guilt about not handling the situation better from the start overwhelmed me at times. Then I remembered Lerner's words again, "A bold act of pretending can help expand what is real and true about ourselves and our relationships."[39]

I could act as if I were calm about this, I could pretend I had the courage to deal with it head on, and I could be clear about my part in it. I could speak from my heart and not my head. I could acknowledge that I made a mistake, that I was worried about the impact of a dog on our lives, and that I should have realized this sooner. I could find my voice, and I could stay connected.

I'd like to say that I had enough skill to resolve the issue quickly after settling on that strategy. But it took a few more weeks. And despite trying to act as if I was calm and courageous in the face of a difficult conversation, at times I felt awkward. It felt easier to get irritated and to point out the ridiculousness of having a dog, considering everything else going on in our lives. When I did that, it temporarily strained our connection, and I had to work hard to patch up the part of the blanket that was fraying. I knew that while I handled the situation poorly at times, there is a purpose for every conversation. There is an opportunity for learning, a reason that things happen the way they do. I was able to practice the skill of deepening a connection through authentic conversation. And after the difficulty and disappointment, we found a compromise. We got a cat when we returned home. She fits well into our lifestyle, we both love and enjoy her, and she makes us feel more connected as a family.

ACTION: Think about a difficult conversation that you need to have. Develop a strategy that allows you to stay connected with the other person while staying true to the message you want to deliver.

REFLECTION: How did it go? What happened to the quality of your connection with the person both in the moment and over time? What part of your strategy worked best? What would you do differently next time?

"Realize deeply that the present moment is all you ever have."[40] **- Eckhart Tolle**

So what gets in the way of connection? My ability to stay focused on the present moment has a drastic impact on the quality of my connection with the people I'm with and with the world around me. In the fourth week of the trip, I worked hard to pay attention to the little things instead of constantly planning what we would do next. As we arrived in Yosemite, I

> *"I think a sense of right relatedness and connection is every . . .. person's ultimate desire."*
> Bernie, Maryland, USA

noticed the beautiful scenery, the vibrant colors, and the warmth of the sun. We sat in the sun for the rest of the afternoon, moving from the indoor pool to the outdoor pool depending on how hot we felt. During dinner that evening, we looked through the photos on my iPhone, reminding ourselves of all the fantastic things we'd done so far. We relaxed, and we didn't rush off to do the next thing. I knew it was a luxury to have the time to stay grounded and connected. As Brené Brown says, "We are a culture of people who've bought into the idea that if we stay busy enough, the truth of our lives won't catch up with us."[41]

I tried hard to use this time to connect with everything around me and to enhance my connection with Josh. While I tried not to be in my head, planning the next thing, I wasn't always successful. It is difficult to break the habits of a lifetime. It was in one of those less successful moments, in the middle of Yosemite, that Josh asked, "Mom, how do you think they run?" I didn't know who "they" were, although I had heard him chattering about something in the background. I thought maybe it was about animals or perhaps super heroes. So I took a shot . . . "do you mean the super monkey?" I knew I'd missed the mark by a pretty wide margin when he replied with, "Never MIND!"

Immediately the connection was compromised. The blanket was strained, his enthusiasm about the topic had dampened, and I had disappointed him. What had I been thinking about that was so important that I couldn't stay focused when my son was telling me something that he was clearly interested in? Nothing.

I identified with something Paulo Coelho writes in his book *The Pilgrimage,* "The world was there around me, and I realized that seldom had I paid attention to it."[42] I apologized to Josh, told him I really did want to know what he was talking about, and said that I knew it might not seem that way to him. It took a while before he would explain it to me and before we could tighten the weave of the strained blanket once more.

REFLECTION: Reflect on times when you are not fully present. What causes you not to be present? How does that affect those around you? What judgments do you have of yourself at these times?

ACTION: Using the information from your reflection, develop a strategy for staying present more often. How did it go? How did that influence the quality of your connection with others?

Later that week, as I told Ann about my failure to be fully present with Josh, we had the following conversation:

Karen: One of the interesting things I've noticed this week is that when I'm not fully present it has a negative effect on connection.
Ann: What do you mean?
Karen: Well, I'm in my head such a lot of the time, planning the next thing or calculating how long each activity will take to make sure it fits into the day. While I'm doing that, I'm not paying attention to what's going on in the moment.

> *"I can sometimes get worried that if I tell a friend personal things about myself, they might laugh. But then I miss out on the opportunity for a great friendship and a great connection with that person"*
> *Stacy, Virginia, USA*

Ann: Well, what if that is your way of connecting? You might simply have a different approach than other people. And just as with all approaches to life, sometimes it works and sometimes it doesn't.

"Connection is the energy created between people when they feel seen, heard, and valued; when they can give and receive without judgment,"[43] as Brown defines it in *Daring Greatly.* Ann's perspective on connection made me think. I had been so busy judging myself that I hadn't tried to reframe the situation in a positive light. How satisfying it was to have someone understand and accept who I am. My connection with Ann grew stronger, along with my own self-acceptance.

> **REFLECTION:**   Reflect on times when you are fully present. What is different about those situations that allow you to stay present? What does being present feel like?

> **ACTION:**   How can you use this information to create a strategy for staying present more often? Practice some more. What did you learn about yourself?

∽

"You cannot belong to anyone else, until you belong to yourself."[44] **- Pearl Bailey**

One of the most interesting conversations I had with Josh during the whole trip was during the week we focused on connection. We started talking about being ourselves and being true to who we are.

Josh: I am never fully myself, I wish I could be who I really am with everyone, my sometimes weirdo self.

Karen: Oh that's a shame – why do you feel like you can't be yourself?

> *"That's why you really have to remember that you really should be proud of who you are! Be proud of the things you're good at and the things you like to do for fun, even if it's different from everybody else."*
>
> *Stacy, Virginia, USA*

Josh: Because I've got to fit in, and people have to like me.

Karen: Oh – I think you've really just been talking about connection, and the need to feel like you belong.

Josh: Huh . . really? Wow, I never knew that!

Karen: Do you feel like you're not fully yourself with me?

Josh: Duh . . no . . you're my mom.

Later in the trip he talked about the importance of popularity at school, describing the social hierarchy in terms of circles. In the inner circle, there were only a few kids, but they were the most popular. Then there was the middle circle, with kids who were reasonably popular, but not as popular as those in the inner circle. Finally, there was the outer circle of the least popular kids. I was fascinated. It brought back feelings from my own childhood about how important it was to fit in, to be liked, to be part of the in crowd. "Belonging is the innate human desire to be part of something larger than us . . . We often try to acquire it by fitting in and by seeking approval, which are not only hollow substitutes for belonging, but often barriers to it,"[45] Brown writes.

I felt sad that it was so important for Josh to be liked that he felt couldn't always be completely himself. And yet I understood it, remembered it, connected with the feeling. I also knew that my strongest and longest lasting connections are with the people with whom I can truly be myself, and that when I am not myself

> *"We were each made with a very unique personality and very unique likes and dislikes . . . so we're not SUPPOSED to be like other people!"*
>
> *Stacy, Virginia, USA*

the connections are shallow. In the end you can only be who you are. Brown continues, "Because true belonging only happens when we present our authentic, imperfect selves to the world, our sense of belonging can never be greater than our level of self acceptance"[46]

REFLECTION: Reflect on the extent to which you are truly yourself with everyone you know. Who do you mold yourself for? How do you adjust yourself to try to fit in?

ACTION: Take a risk. In the situations that you've identified above, show up as your authentic self. Be who you truly are. What happens? How do you feel about yourself? What happens to your sense of belonging?

As the week drew to a close, I reflected on how vital connection is to our sense of well-being. It is the foundation of our existence, the thread that connects us with something larger than ourselves. It's also easily torn, and there is

> *"I think when people feel connected they are happier and it raises their self esteem and self confidence."*
>
> *Fiona, England*

work required to patch it. It grows with kindness, respect and acceptance. It withers with judgment, disapproval, and isolation. As I looked forward to next week's theme of empathy, I recognized that empathy creates connection. In the words of Brown, "Empathy is . . emotionally connecting, and communicating that incredibly healing message of 'You're not alone'."[47]

Complete the following sentences:

1. For me, connection means ....

2. I feel most connected when ....

3. When I am connected I feel ....

4. The things that make me feel disconnected include ....

5. Being disconnected feels ....

Josh's Journal

Week 5

July 21st, 2012
Today I went indoor sky diving and to the beach. Sweet!

July 22nd, 2012
Today I went on a hike to Mount Tam. Nice.

July 23rd, 2012
Today I went from the Bay Area to Crescent City.

July 24th, 2012
I went to Portland and saw a soccer game. It was awesome. Villa won 7-6.

July 25th, 2012
I went into Portland and went to the Maritime Museum and had a voodoo doughnut and went on the aerial tram. Beast!

July 26th, 2012
I went in the Seattle Space Needle today. Sweet!

Empathy

Week 5: Seattle, Washington; via Portland, Oregon; San Francisco Bay Area and Crescent City, California.

Total mileage so far: 6,177.

Theme for Week 5: Empathy.

> **"Seeing with the eyes of another, listening with the ears of another, and feeling with the heart of another."**[48] **- Alfred Adler**

I knew our week was off to a less than auspicious start after our first conversation about empathy.

> **Karen**: So, Josh, our theme for this week is Empathy. Do you know what that is?
> **Josh**: No idea!
> **Karen**: Well, it's when you can put yourself in someone else's shoes and imagine what they're experiencing.
> **Josh**: Well, you're on your own this week, Mom, because I have no idea what you're talking about!

Despite the relationship between connection and empathy that had emerged the week before, it turned out that empathy is complicated. I thought it was simply the ability to imagine what someone else is feeling. If you are able to do that, your connection with that person increases. I realized that while that's true, it is only part of it. Empathy requires practice, a

> *"[Empathy is] an ability to tune into and relate to someone's thoughts, emotions, problems, aspirations."*
>
> *Jean, England*

different way of listening, and a new way of responding to people. If we're not careful, we interpret how others are feeling based on what we would feel, inserting our story into their situation and our response. And I realized there are times when it is difficult to have empathy. It's hard to avoid the temptation to solve people's problems, and it's hard to feel empathy when the other person isn't kind.

As we drove over the Golden Gate Bridge at the start of the week, my spirits lifted with memories of living in San Francisco. The sky was blue; the light sparkled. We pulled over to look across the bay at the city, with Alcatraz in the middle of the bay and the Transamerica Pyramid standing out among the tall buildings in the skyline. We continued the drive along the hilly streets of Mill Valley, winding through the redwood trees and passing houses built on stilts buried into the hillside. Josh was excited that we were going to stay with a family that had more kids. I was excited to see Sabine again, along with her husband, Vic, and her children, Hannah and Lorenz. We would have the chance to look back on times when we shared an apartment in San Francisco many years ago and to catch up on where our lives were today.

Stephen Covey uses the metaphor of an Emotional Bank Account to describe the amount of trust that is built up in a relationship. "Empathic listening is the key to making deposits in Emotional Bank Accounts." [49] Sabine and I were able to reconnect and pick up where we left off because the earlier deposits in our Emotional Bank Accounts were still there. We spent the weekend building on those and reestablishing our connection and friendship. As Josh and I paid attention to empathy throughout the week, it was clear that there is more to empathy than simply listening. Our Emotional Bank Account balances went up and down. Sometimes we put deposits in; other times we made unintentional withdrawals. We spent the week practicing empathy, and we learned a lot. And as I sat down to write this book, I realized that I still have more to learn.

⁂

"Imagining what it is like to be someone other than yourself is at the core of our humanity."[50] - Ian McEwan

Practicing empathy requires imagination. This week we looked for opportunities to imagine what life is like from someone else's perspective.

It was surprisingly difficult. As we waited in line with Sabine and her family for brunch in Mill Valley, watching as tables that were not quite big enough for us were given to others, I became increasingly irritated. I sighed every time the host said it wouldn't be long and then again when smaller groups were seated ahead of us. And then I caught myself. I tried to imagine what it would be like if I were the host and a slightly annoyed English

> *"A new perspective allows me to change my thoughts or patterns of behavior."*
> Ann, California, USA

woman asked multiple times how long the wait would be. When I put myself in his shoes, I could see the impact I was having more clearly. I realized how frustrating it must be for him. It gave me pause, and I decided change my behavior. I smiled, apologized, and said that it must be challenging to manage such a large line and keep everyone happy. He smiled back cautiously, no doubt suspicious of my change in attitude. Finally we were seated, and brunch was worth the wait. What was the balance in my Emotional Bank Account with the host? Probably around zero, but at least it was not in the red as it had been earlier. While I would never see him again, I thought about how I had a much more positive effect on others and felt much better when I brought empathy into the interaction.

Later that week in Portland, we went to a soccer game. The game was particularly exciting because the Portland Timbers were playing Aston Villa F.C., a team my father supports in the UK. Josh was especially enthusiastic – he loves going to watch sports in general, and soccer in particular. The skies were blue, the weather was a sunny and comfortable seventy-five degrees, and Josh was going to support Villa.

As we walked to our section, I realized that I had unknowingly booked seats with a restricted view. The stadium wasn't crowded, so we decided to sit at the other end of the row. If people who had booked those seats arrived, we would move. The game started, the seats slowly filled up, and some people arrived and sat in our original seats. Clearly they hadn't checked their tickets properly. I mentioned this quietly to Josh, who was engrossed in the game, cheering and adding commentary. I said I was going to tell them that we were in their seats. In a panic, he said, "Shush, Mom, don't do that. I like these seats." I went ahead anyway. They were grateful to get a much better view, and we went up a couple of rows to empty seats where we could see perfectly.

We discussed what happened when we went to get drinks at half time.

Karen: So, while we're on empathy, can you imagine how you would feel if you were those people and you realized at the end of the game that someone else had been in your seats, and you hadn't been able to see part of the game?

Josh: Ooooooh, now I see what you mean, I'd have felt bad . . .

Karen: And you might have been angry too, right?

Josh: Oh yeah . . .

> *"I think empathy is the ability to put yourself in someone else's shoes and walk around."*
> *Ann, California, USA*

Opportunities to practice empathy present themselves every day. They occur in our most basic interactions with others, often with people we will never see again. They also show up in our most important relationships, where the balances in our Emotional Bank Accounts have more influence on our everyday lives. Practicing empathy in less risky, lower-profile situations, with people that we won't see again, helps us develop the empathy we need to bring to our more significant relationships. In both types of situations we become kinder people with a more positive impact, people who know how to build connections.

REFLECTION: Next time you are irritated with someone, try to Pause, Reflect, and Choose (PRC).

1. Pause to observe yourself and see how you might be affecting the situation.
2. Reflect on what might be going on for the other person and imagine how he or she might feel.
3. Choose a different response, one that shows empathy and therefore makes a deposit in your Emotional Bank Account with this person.

ACTION: Practice this over the next week and see how many times you remember to do it. Then notice how many times you choose a different behavior or reaction.

How does this influence your relationship with the person? How do you feel about yourself at the end of the week?

You may complete this exercise and all the exercises in the chapter in the exercise section at the back of the book and share your observations on my blog at: http://worklifeperspectives.com/Life_is_a_Road_Trip_.html

ᕲᕲ

"The great gift of human beings is that we have the power of empathy, we can all sense a mysterious connection to each other."[51] Meryl Streep

One of the great things about having a GPS is that you never really get lost. One of the downsides is that you can't quite visualize where you are at any single point in time, or how far you have to go. I was in this situation as we headed toward the Oregon border during a marathon two days at the wheel, which totaled more than thirteen hours of driving. Tired and dispirited, with the car running low on gas, I asked Josh to pull out the map for me. I needed to work out how soon we might reach a gas station. Josh, who was also irritable with the boredom of such long car journeys and in an unhelpful mood, said something sarcastic. I felt overwhelmed, my feelings were hurt, and the tears welled. I paused. Josh didn't seem at all aware of the impact his statement had, and so I decided to use this as a teaching moment.

> *"I think that empathy is one of our most important qualities."*
> Aileen, North Carolina, USA

Karen: Since this week is about empathy, I'd like you to sit and think for ten minutes about how it might feel to be me when you respond with a sarcastic comment, when all I asked for was some help.
Josh: Ten minutes? That's ages.
Karen: Yes, it is. We'll continue driving, and I will do the same and think about what you're going through at the moment.
Josh: OK.

This was actually difficult for me to do. I dwelled on how tired I was, vaguely aware that he was too, and I knew that the balances in our Emotional Bank Accounts were at risk of being depleted. Ten minutes later, we discussed it some more.

Karen: Well, what did you come up with?

Josh: I think you feel bad . . I think you feel that I'm not a good navigator and texter (a role he assigned for himself).

Karen: Yes, I do feel bad, because I felt hurt that when I asked for some help what I got was a sarcastic response.

Josh: Oh, I'm sorry, now I feel bad, why am I sarcastic? I don't know . . . Oh I feel horrible . . . I shouldn't be sarcastic.

Karen: Well, what ideas do you have about why you might have responded with sarcasm?

Josh: I don't know . . . I'm sorry.

Karen: That's OK. I am thinking that just as it's hard for me to do all this driving, it's also hard for you to do all this sitting. Was it hard to put yourself in someone else's shoes and figure out how they were feeling?

Josh: Yes, really hard.

Karen: Do you think it would get easier if you practiced it more?

Josh: Oh definitely.

While our conversation may not exactly meet Covey's criteria of empathic listening, it allowed us to continue practicing empathy. It also helped us stay connected during two days of a lot of driving. Brené Brown says, "Empathy is connecting with the emotion that someone is experiencing, not the event or the circumstance."[52] Later in the day, it became clear that our conversation had created the space for Josh to contemplate, and then articulate, what he was really feeling.

Josh: What is homesick?

Karen: It means you miss home, your friends, etc.

Josh: Mom, I think I've figured out why I'm being grumpy and sarcastic.

Karen: Why is that?

Josh : I think I'm homesick.

Karen: Oh I see. I'm sorry; I can totally understand that. It's OK to be homesick.

Josh: Yes, that's it, that's how I feel.

Karen: Well, we've done a big trip, there's been a lot of

> *"Sometimes I am surprised at how another experiences a similar emotion. It gives me more depth and breadth of my own experience."*
>
> Ann, California, USA

loading and unloading, and we haven't stayed in any single place very long. It's not surprising that we're both feeling a bit tired and grumpy at this point is it?

Josh: No – this has really been a big trip. I miss my home and my room and my friends.

Karen: I know; it's OK.

Josh: Sorry for being sarcastic, Mom.

Karen: That's OK. I understand how you feel.

There are many other ways the conversation could have gone. If I hadn't been mindful of empathy this week, I might not have paused before reacting to his sarcasm. I might have become stuck in my feelings of irritation and responded with anger. Had I done so, our connection would have become strained. Instead we both made deposits in each other's Emotional Bank Account. And, in the end, as the fuel indicator got closer to empty, we pulled together as a team in search of a gas station.

Josh caught himself every time he was sarcastic that day, even when his intention was humorous. We talked about how tricky the line is between sarcasm that is funny and sarcasm that is hurtful. However, I realized that while we learned a lot from the conversations, exhaustion kept me from calling on my empathy as quickly as I would have liked. Clearly this week was more challenging than I thought!

REFLECTION: Think back on a conversation that you had recently with someone significant in your life where your lack of empathy put your Emotional Bank Account into the red. How could you have approached the situation differently?

ACTION: Make a deposit in your Emotional Bank Account with that person. How does it affect the quality of your connection with them?

ᖉ

"Seeking first to understand, diagnosing before you prescribe, is hard."[53] **- Stephen Covey**

On our last day in the Bay Area, we hiked on Mount Tamalpais. As we drove up the mountain on tiny roads with hairpin bends, we moved into the fog. The temperature gauge dropped down to the low fifties. As we moved through the fog and out the other side, the temperature moved steadily back in to the seventies. When we finally emerged at the top, we looked down on a blanket of fog; it looked like a huge soft cotton ball.

> *"Sometimes I wonder if my concern is also their concern."*
> *John, Virginia, USA*

We hiked for about an hour in the beautiful sunshine. Josh was in a grumpy mood, snapping at me and not wanting me to be near him. I tried to figure out what might be going on, wondering if being with a larger more traditional family than ours was hard for him or made him feel sad. And then I realized that I might be projecting those things as I viewed him through my own filters. Later, I asked him about it.

Karen: So how do you feel when you stay with a family like Sabine's?
Josh: I don't know. Who did you like best, Hannah or Lorenz?
Karen: I like them both equally. So how do you feel about being around that kind of family?
Josh: I think Lorenz and Hannah are equal. I don't know. I'm going to read.

Clearly open-ended questions weren't working. I decided to change my strategy and try again.

Karen: So when you're with a family like Sabine's, do you feel sad that ours isn't like that?

Josh: Yes.

Karen: Is that why you were a bit grumpy on Sunday?

Josh: Yes, maybe. I'm going to read again.

Frustrated, I realized that neither approach was working. And then I recalled something Covey wrote, "Probing is playing twenty questions. It's autobiographical, it controls, and it invades."[54] I was bringing my own story to this conversation, my own worry that Josh would prefer to be in a larger family. I was also probing, not giving him the time to process his feelings and open up. I wanted to talk to him about it, and I didn't ask whether he wanted to do the same.

I never really found out what made him grumpy. My initial assessment might have been right, but he could have been tired, or it could have been something completely different. Maybe he was becoming a teenager, something new and challenging I would have to figure out how to navigate. I know, though, that inserting my story

> *"However, to be truly empathetic I must leave my own experience and be open to theirs"*
>
> Ann, California, USA

didn't make a deposit in our Emotional Bank Account; it didn't enhance our connection. "The most important deposit you could make would be just to listen, without . . . reading your own autobiography into what he says,"[55] according to Covey.

REFLECTION: Reflect on a situation where your own story stood in the way of you showing true empathy for someone. How often does this story influence your interpretation of people and events?

ACTION: Develop a strategy for leaving your story behind and for being completely open to putting yourself in the other person's shoes. What is the result? What is the impact on the other person? How does it affect your Emotional Bank Account with them?

"Scholars have called empathy a 'fragile flower,' easily crushed by self-concern."[56]- David Brooks

Drawing on my empathy was not always straightforward, and it turned out to be especially hard toward the end of the Villa game. The game had been exciting. Josh had been describing strategies to me, observing the skills of the players, and distinguishing the American team's style of play from that of the English team. He was insightful and full of commentary. He wasn't loud or critical, and he wasn't shouting, pushing, or making trouble. He was a typical ten-year-old boy who was thoroughly enjoying the game. I was enamored by his insights and energized by his enthusiasm.

When Villa scored their first goal, we both cheered, and the person in front of us turned around and shushed us. When Villa scored their second goal, Josh was beside himself with excitement. The same person turned around and asked Josh to be quiet. Without thinking, I said, "He's ten, and he's enjoying the game. Are you going to tell everyone else to be quiet too?" My instinct was immediately to jump to my son's defense. I could tell Josh felt bad, and I told him not to let it spoil the game. If he'd been loud and unruly, I would have been the first to ask him to calm down. But he wasn't. He was being delightful. I was hurt by her unkindness, and my empathy for her was nowhere to be found.

On the train ride home, Josh and I talked about her reaction and he was indignant. My overwhelming feeling was to want to protect him. I didn't want someone else's words to hurt him, for him to feel bad about himself, or for his enthusiasm to be dampened. I told him that if he'd been behaving badly I would have reacted differently, but because he wasn't, I felt the same indignation.

We did briefly discuss what might have been going on for her: Perhaps she'd had a bad day at work; perhaps she wasn't a mother and was not used to the energy and enthusiasm of ten-year-old boys; perhaps she didn't like crowds. While I considered her point of view in the spirit of our theme of empathy, it seemed like lip service and was not truly heartfelt. Perhaps if I had

> *"I always encourage my children to consider others' feelings and that we never know what cross they are carrying, even while trying to understand even the most bizarre and irrational behaviors."*
>
> *Aileen, North Carolina, USA*

put more effort into it, there would have been a powerful lesson for both of us about being empathetic even when you're feeling threatened and defensive. However, it felt much more important to give Josh the message that I was in his corner than to practice empathy with someone I didn't know. I needed to place a large deposit in my Emotional Bank Account with Josh; I didn't need to be concerned about the negative balance in my account with a stranger.

> **REFLECTION**: What situations make you feel defensive, threatened, and protective of yourself, your family, and your friends? How does that affect your ability to show empathy?

> **ACTION**: In the future, try to show empathy with the other person in one of those situations. What did you learn about yourself? Would you do anything differently in the future?

As we drove toward Seattle on the last day of the week, I suggested to Josh that we conclude by each saying how we thought the other person was feeling about the trip at that point.

> **Josh**: I think you are thinking that I'm a bad person because I've been very sarcastic the last few days and that I'm not doing a very good job as navigator/texter.
> **Karen**: Oh no, Josh. I don't think you're a bad person. I am certainly feeling a little tired from the driving and moving from one place to another so often, but my primary feeling is not that you're bad. I'm so sorry that you think that.

"Nothing you do is a deposit unless the other person perceives it as such,"[57] Covey says. I realized that despite my best efforts to make deposits in his Emotional bank Account, Josh remembered something different. He didn't remember that I told him what a great job he was doing with the traveling and that I thanked him for packing up his suitcase and remembering to put his dirty laundry in the right place. He remembered that I told him he hurt my feelings. He remembered me being tired and irritable from driving. He remembered the story he told himself, that he's a bad texter and navigator. So while we practiced empathy this week, it didn't have quite the impact that I hoped, at least not in that moment. Perhaps it created a foundation for the future, one that he can build on.

Then, I took my turn to see if I knew how he was feeling about the trip.

Karen: I'm thinking that you're enjoying it, but that it's hard to sit in the car for the long drives, and they're a bit boring, and that it's hard not having other kids around.

Josh: Yes, that's pretty much about right.

As the fifth week ended, the relationship between the themes became illuminated once more. Being empathetic is difficult, especially when the other person is unkind or when you feel threatened. When you're able to practice empathy and the other person is able to receive it, the impact is positive. The connection between two people increases, and a deposit is made in your relationship's Emotional Bank Account.

> *"To acknowledge and allow someone to own their feelings is powerful and very important. Regardless of them being right or wrong."*
>
> Aileen, North Carolina, USA

In the sixth week, we would have the opportunity to use the lessons of empathy to build on our skills of collaboration. Because as Covey says, "If you want to interact effectively with me . . you first need to understand me." [58]

Complete the following sentences:

1. Imagining how someone else feels is .... because
   ....

2. Showing empathy results in.........................

3. It's hardest to imagine how someone else feels when
   ....

4. When I show empathy I learn that.........................

5. If someone shows me empathy I feel ....

Josh's Journal

Week 6

July 27th, 2012
Today I did the Family Fun Center, shot a BB gun, and learned to fly fish.

July 28th, 2012
Today I went on a paddle boat around Lake Union.

July 29th, 2012
Today I went to the mall and rock climbing. Cool!

July 30th, 2012
Today I went to the Riverfront Park in Spokane and saw Brave the movie. And I played mini-golf.

July 31st, 2012
Today I went and saw *Ice Age: Continental Drift*. It was a good movie.

August 1st, 2012
Today I went to Yellowstone National Park and went to a place called Mammoth Hot Springs. It was amazing.

Collaboration

Week 6: Yellowstone National Park, Wyoming; via Seattle and Spokane, Washington; and Helena, Montana.

Total mileage so far: 6,965.

Theme for Week 6: Collaboration.

> **"Coming together is a beginning, staying together is progress, working together is success."[59] - Henry Ford**

I let Josh choose the theme for the sixth week.

Karen: So Josh would you like to choose our theme for next week? What do you prefer – collaboration or courage?
Josh: What does collaboration mean?
Karen: Well, it means working together with people, a bit like working in a team.
Josh: Oh – then collaboration.
Karen: OK – what made you choose that?
Josh: Well, we're going to stay with Sebastian, so we'll be doing stuff together, so that will be collaboration.

Josh and I had been collaborating for the past five weeks, sometimes more successfully than others. The sixth week presented an opportunity to think about how to collaborate well and about what interferes with collaboration. As had been the case at the start of other

> *"I see collaboration as working together to obtain shared goals."*
>
> Orla, Northern Ireland

weeks, we noticed the connection between our new theme and the prior themes. To collaborate well, you have to be able to understand where the other person is coming from, what their interests are, and what motivates them. Empathy is critical in gaining that understanding. Showing kindness encourages more collaboration, the impact is positive, the connection enhanced. All the themes continued to weave together.

In their book *Radical Collaboration*, James W. Tamm and Ronald J. Luyet use a Green Zone and Red Zone framework to identify behaviors that encourage collaboration as opposed to those that hinder it, as shown in the chart that follows. "Individuals in the Green Zone convey an authentic non-defensive presence, while those in the Red Zone convey defensiveness and fear."[60] As the week passed, there were times when we were in the Green Zone, times when we were in the Red Zone, and times when we were somewhere between the two.

Someone in the Green Zone...	Someone in the Red Zone...
Takes and accept responsibility	Distances from responsibility
Responds non-defensively	Responds defensively
Is not easily threatened	Feels threatened and wronged
Builds mutual success	Triggers defensiveness in others
Seeks solutions not blame	Blames and accuses others
Uses persuasion not force	Creates a climate of antagonism
Is firm, but not rigid	Is rigid, reactive, righteous
Thinks short and long term	Focuses on short term gain/win
Is interested in other perspectives	Feels victimized by different perspectives
Welcomes feedback	Does not seek or value feedback
Sees conflict as natural	Sees conflict as a battle to be won
Talks calmly about difficult issues	Communicates disapproval and contempt
Has a caring attitude	Shows Black/white, right/wrong thinking
Sees excellence over victory	Sees others as the enemy
Listens well	Does not listen well

"Individually we are one drop. Together we are an ocean."[61]
- Ryunosuke Satoro

At the start of the sixth week, we arrived in Seattle to stay with friends. I met Clare more than twenty years ago when we worked together in London. I had stayed with her and her husband, Kaj, for a few months in

San Francisco while I found a job and a place to live. Their son, Sebastian, is a year older than Josh. Staying with them was like going home. Everything was familiar, and we laughed and joked about things from the past. We updated each other on our lives and the lives of people we knew in common. We felt like we were with family.

As I got up on the first day, I could hear a heated conversation coming from the basement where the boys were playing with Sebastian's Xbox. I knew they were trying to collaborate when I heard Josh shout, "No, I want to play on your team, otherwise you'll cream me!" Collaboration started that morning firmly in the Red Zone, with the focus on how to win, or at least how not to lose too badly!

After that ominous start, we decided to visit a nearby amusement center that had a plethora of activities, including mini golf, laser tag, arcade machines, and go-karts. Josh and Sebastian loved it. I tolerated it, knowing I would get a mental break for the day. Clare and Kaj were relieved to be at work. All of our interests were met. I bought a package that gave them a certain number of tickets to use. I watched them collaborate on how to use their tickets, deciding which activities to do and what they would have to forfeit.

As I watched them, it reminded me of how Bruce Tuckman describes a team that first comes together, where everyone is a little cautious and on their best behavior, not wanting to be rejected by the group.[62] Josh and Sebastian were both very much in the Green Zone. They listened to each other so that they could understand what the other was interested in doing, and

> "When you want to collaborate with someone . . . you have to be willing to listen to someone else's ideas and respect them and work together to come up with creative solutions together."
>
> Stacy, Virginia, USA

they came to agreements over common interests. They were firm but not rigid about their preferences, occasionally coming in to conflict and then finding a resolution. When necessary, they used persuasion, discussing options calmly rather than getting aggressive or angry. And for one of the activities, they decided they would each do something different, rather than having to agree to do the same. Both of them seemed pleased with the outcome. I was relieved watching them, knowing the skills they displayed would be crucial as they got older. As Tamm and Luyet write, "The world has become far too complex and interrelated for individuals to succeed without collaborative skills"[63]

At the end of the day, we visited the arcade. Every game they played could earn them tickets, depending on their score, and they chose the games with the greatest likelihood of spitting out a lot of tickets. More tickets means more prizes. When they finished the games, they tallied up their tickets, and Josh had more than Sebastian. Continuing the spirit of collaboration, Josh suggested that they pool the tickets. They looked at the prizes and negotiated about what to get. They went back and forth, still in the Green Zone, suggesting options, excluding them, explaining why they preferred one thing instead of another. They finally agreed on a plastic mini-dart toy for each and some candy.

"The Green Zone gives individuals the attitude and a state of mind that allows them to focus their energy and skills on creative problem solving," according to Tamm and Luyet.[64] Staying in the Green Zone for the day meant they had each done the things that were most important to them. When they disagreed on something, they solved the problem creatively and agreed on how to proceed. It seemed like they had moved through their conflicts with the intuitive knowledge that conflict contributes to collaboration if handled in the right way. At times they become a little competitive, but they always moved back to Green Zone behaviors. As a result we had a great, fun-filled day, and both boys ended up with prizes!

ACTION: Identify someone with whom you feel safe to ask for feedback on your own collaborative skills. Show them the list of Green Zone and Red Zone behaviors and ask them to tell you how you fare in each category.

REFLECTION: Reflect on their feedback. Was it what you were expecting? What was the biggest surprise? What behavior could you change in order to get better results in future?

You may complete this exercise and all the exercises in the chapter in the exercise section at the back of the book and share your observations on my blog at: http://worklifeperspectives. com/Life_is_a_Road_Trip_.html

"How about the opening of the Olympics - surely the biggest collaboration of all!"

Jean, England

When I gave Josh the option of collaboration or courage as a theme, I hadn't even been thinking that the Olympic Games were about to begin. After our day at the amusement center, we watched the opening ceremony on TV. We were excited to see the pageantry and the shots of London and to be watching it with another British family. As I reflected on the Olympics, I realized that there was a curious mix of concepts that relate to collaboration.

- **Conflict**: When the Games started in ancient Greece, the city-states agreed to postpone all conflicts for the period of the games. To collaborate successfully, it's essential to be able to move through conflict, which can lead to consensus if handled skillfully.
- **Competition**. In the Games, there are winners and losers, a medal table to keep score, and great excitement for the winning nation. Competition is win-lose; collaboration is win-win. Developing the skills to move from competition into collaboration is crucial to building successful relationships and teams. And being able to collaborate internally as a team, staying focused on the common goal rather than trying to outdo each other, is vital for successfully competing against others.
- **Compromise**. Later in the year, I attended a presentation delivered by one of the organizers of the Games. He described how crucial compromise was to the successful completion of the new stadiums that hosted the Games. Compromise is more of a lose a bit-lose a bit situation, and is often the route taken when it's not possible to reach a win-win solution.[65] Developing the skills to compromise and collaborate is important in all areas of life. Knowing when to move from one to the other is critical in obtaining the outcomes needed in certain situations.

The design and execution of the opening ceremony alone was clearly an enormous exercise in collaboration, with a spectacular end result. We watched in awe at the creativity of tributes to different periods in British history. We were excited as David Beckham brought in the flame and passed it to seven junior athletes, who lit the cauldron. The Guardian newspaper summarized it beautifully:

"So in the end, the cauldron is not lit by a lone Olympian from the past, but by seven teenagers whose days of glory are surely yet to come. The torches ignite the copper petals; the petals in turn ignite the cauldron. It is a masterstroke, a dazzling end to a night of wonders and a glorious salute to the democratic spirit of Olympics; enshrining these games as a collective endeavour and a celebration of emerging talent."[66]

In his opening speech, Lord Sebastian Coe said, "No one person . . . is enough to get the complexity of this project across the line."[67] It's inconceivable to think this could have been done by one person or even by one group. As the old African proverb says, "If you want to go fast, go alone. If you want to go far, go together."[68]

REFLECTION: Think of a time when you successfully collaborated as part of a team. What worked well? What challenges did you face? How did you overcome them? What was the end result? What was your contribution to the collaboration?

ACTION: The next time you have the opportunity to collaborate, take the lessons learned from your reflection and apply them. What is the outcome?

༄

"The strength of the team is each individual member. The strength of each member is the team."[69] - Phil Jackson

Not long after we arrived in Seattle, Clare said to me, "So, I was thinking we would go to Home Depot on Sunday." It might seem like a strange proposal for someone on an eight-week road trip, but one of my passions is decorating houses. I had helped Clare paint her apartment in San Francisco, and she regularly asked me for advice with colors, tiles, floors, etc. I was excited. I love to put colors

"Some people are better at a process than you are, and you may be able to contribute where they cannot- that is the best of collaboration."

Ann, California, USA

together – it's one of the few creative talents I have, despite being surrounded by a family of artists.

As we got ready to leave, Clare pulled out her binder. She wanted to redecorate a bathroom, and she had separate sections for floors, walls, paints, and tiles. She had noted costs of different options, contact names, and quotes for different aspects of the work. It was as organized as the multi-tab spreadsheet I had created for the trip and probably more detailed. I spent some time listening to her describe her vision for the bathroom. She created the agenda for our visit to Home Depot, and I would contribute ideas and develop the color scheme.

When we arrived, I found a beautiful multicolored glass tile that looked like a mosaic and matched the sink she'd bought. We had a foundation for the design. I picked up different paint chips, held them up to the floor samples, and we assessed whether they matched. We looked at showerheads and faucets. We considered so many variables that at one point Clare said, "This is the point where I normally go home because there are too many choices." I knew what she meant, but this is one of the activities where I don't get overwhelmed with creative ideas. After an hour or so we left with ideas formulated and options chosen. She had translated her vision into a plan that she could execute.

Clare's research meant that we knew what to look for, that we didn't miss anything or waste any time, and that we considered the alternatives before making final decisions. I had provided the creative perspective and my experience from decorating the five houses I'd owned and from helping friends with their homes. By bringing our different skills, experiences, ideas and strengths, we ensured the bathroom would come out better than if either one of us had been on our own.

> *"When you want to collaborate with someone . . . you have to be willing to listen to someone else's ideas and respect them and work together to come up with creative solutions together."*
>
> Stacy, Virginia, USA

REFLECTION: Think of a team or group that you have recently been part of where you were working toward a goal. A team is two or more people. What are the strengths, skills, and experience you bring to the team? Where do you commonly rely on the strengths and skills of others to fill gaps?

ACTION: Write down the list of strengths that you and each of your team members contribute to the success of the team. To what extent are you leveraging everyone's strengths to the fullest? What adjustments can you make in people's roles to increase their contribution? How can you use this strategy for teams that you are part of in the future?

∾

"Collaboration, it turns out, is not a gift from the Gods, but a skill that requires effort and practice."[70] - Douglas B Reeves

As we drove away from Seattle toward Spokane, Josh and I revisited his choice of theme.

Karen: So, you chose collaboration because we were going to Clare's house and you'd be collaborating with Sebastian. How do you think it went?
Josh: Sometimes good and sometimes bad.
Karen: Ah – what made it good, and what made it bad? Tell me more.
Josh: Well, it was good when we were playing Xbox together, but it was bad when I accidentally killed him (in the game).

Well, yes, that would do it! We were back on our own again, having stayed with the last of our friends. The rest of the trip would be spent in hotels. Collaboration was down to Josh and me. The four-hour drive to Spokane through the mountains, by the lakes, and along fields of yellow wheat was beautiful. I love arriving in new cities, exploring them, and figuring out the street naming or numbering system. We only had an afternoon in Spokane, and we had to figure out how to spend our time. A river runs through the city, and it also has a number of art galleries, shops, and a nicely laid out downtown area that is easy to walk around. Spokane also has an amusement park with rides, mini golf, arcade games, and more. I was worn out with amusement parks; Josh can never get enough of them. I wanted to walk around the city, browse the shops, and soak in a new place. Walking around a city for the sake of it was not the slightest bit interesting to Josh. We would have to figure out how to collaborate.

Tamm and Luyet write, "Interests are the wants, needs and desires that underlie the problem-solving efforts in the first place."[71] If I were mindful of expressing my interests, and if I understood his, I thought perhaps we could make the situation work for both of us. I remembered an afternoon the prior week that we spent walking from the Portland Aerial Tram back to the center of the town. I hadn't paid enough attention to Josh's interests, which is reflected in the conversation we had during that walk.

> **Josh**: How many blocks are left?
> **Karen**: I think about nine, but look how pretty this is! There's a boardwalk, we can walk right along the river, and we could stop and have a drink, chillax.
> **Josh**: Did you say NINE?
> **Karen**: Yes, I guess I misjudged a bit.
> **Josh**: But NINE? I thought you said half a dozen or so . . . NINE?
> **Karen**: Yes, but let's stop for a drink and have a rest if you like. Look how pretty it is.

I had tried to do what I wanted to do without any input from Josh, and then I was disappointed when he wasn't

> *"To be truly collaborative, you have to be empathetic, able to see all sides of any situation or problem and to negotiate well, know how to defuse heated situations."*
> *Patty, Virginia, USA*

engaged. I shouldn't have been. I decided that I wouldn't let that happen again, especially in a week where I was focused on collaboration. So I resolved to figure out what our interests were.

> **Karen**: We only have a few hours here, and we've already agreed to go and see the movie *Brave* this evening. What would you like to do this afternoon?
> **Josh**: Go to the rides at the Riverfront Park.
> **Karen**: We've been to a lot of amusement parks, and this one doesn't look like one of the best. How about we think about something

different to do today? I'd like to just walk around downtown and see what we see.

Josh: Well, I would really like to go and do the rides.

Karen: What is the reason that's so important to you?

Josh: Because if I don't, I'll miss out on logging a ride in my journal, and I won't be able to give it a score out of ten.

"A surprisingly large number of parties don't even have a good understanding of their own interests, much less the interests of the other side,"[72] Tamm and Luyet write. I had been about to get irritated at the thought of visiting yet another amusement park; I was on the edge of Red Zone defensiveness and criticism. Pausing to obtain a greater understanding of what was motivating Josh and what was important to him moved me back into the Green Zone.

Karen: OK, I understand that's important. I know you're enjoying analyzing everything and keeping a log of that, and I really like your enthusiasm for it.

Josh: Great. Can we go then?

Karen: Yes we can. However, there are some things I would really like to do, too. I really enjoy discovering a new place and getting to know it, and so I'd like to walk around the city a little and then go to the sushi restaurant that has the little plates of sushi on a track that goes around the restaurant.

Josh: Ohhhh, do we have to? I don't like sushi and I don't like shopping.

Karen: I understand that, and I have done a lot more amusement parks than I might normally. I have enjoyed them, but today I'd like to spend some time walking around, because it gives me a feeling of energy to discover a new place.

Josh: OK then, but can we go somewhere else for dinner?

Karen: How many chicken wings have you eaten so far this trip?

"Collaboration is . . . working with people, situations, issues...[to reach]...a narrowing of differences, to the benefit of everyone – whether it is personal, professional, life situation, or relationships."

Patty, Virginia, USA

Josh: Sixty-three (he was logging this in his journal too).

Karen: So how about just for one night we go to sushi? I think it's my turn to choose – don't you?

Josh: I suppose so. Can we go to the amusement park now then?

"A big part of success at collaborative relationships is knowing how to resolve conflicts"[73] We hadn't exactly had an argument, but we had moved in and out of the Green and Red Zones as we navigated the situation and tried to understand where the other was coming from. We had considered each other's interests, and we had created a win-win. We had a lovely afternoon. I had more enthusiasm about the amusement park than I might have otherwise; Josh tolerated walking around Spokane better than he had in Portland. And dinner became a fun activity, too, as we tried to add up the cost of the sushi we were eating based on the quantity and color of the plates we took from the conveyor belt!

REFLECTION: Think of a situation where you have found it difficult to create a win-win situation. Identify the Green Zone and Red Zone behaviors. How would the outcome have been different if you had a clearer idea of your own interests and the interests of others involved?

ACTION: The next time you are finding collaboration challenging, identify the interests of the other parties. If you don't know what they are, ask. How does understanding their interests affect your problem solving skills? What is the outcome?

"As a person becomes more and more defensive, he becomes less and less able to perceive accurately the motives, values and emotions of the sender." [74] - Jack R. Gibb

That evening in Spokane we went to see the movie *Brave*. There was a short, silent film called *La Luna* before the main attraction. It was a story about three generations: a little boy, his father, and his grandfather. The movie is set on the moon, and the little boy joins the family business, where they are responsible for sweeping up fallen stars. In an interview, the creative director describes how he based the movie on his own experience of being caught between these two important figures in his life.[75] You can see the tensions between the father and the grandfather as they each get tied to their own way of sweeping and their own tool. You can see that the little boy is caught in the middle as he tries to navigate the two generations in his family.

"When people get defensive, their thinking becomes rigid, and they are lousy problem solvers,"[76] according to Tamm and Luyet. You don't need words to see defensive behaviors. In this five-minute movie, the negative body language between the father and the grandfather is clear and gets in the way of them being able to work together. The impact on the little boy is palpable. He tries, unsuccessfully, to get them to communicate. There is a struggle over how to move the biggest star, and neither father nor grandfather is able to move it. Both are firmly in the Red Zone, defensive and inflexible. The little boy is the only one able to problem solve; he is the only one who can think of creative approaches to moving the stars. He brings to bear his own tools, his competence, and his patience in looking for another option. And at the end of the movie, he succeeds.

> *"Probably the one thing getting in the way of collaboration is ego!"*
>
> Orla, Northern Ireland

REFLECTION: Reflect on the last time you felt yourself getting defensive. What happens? What are your triggers? Devise a strategy for identifying and managing your triggers earlier in the future.

ACTION: When you feel yourself getting defensive, stop. Recall your strategy, and put it into action. What happens to your ability to collaborate? What is the outcome?

At breakfast the morning after we arrived in Yellowstone National Park, I read parts of an e-mail from a friend of mine who was excited that we had chosen to focus on collaboration.

Josh: Wow, she has really given you a lot of information. That's a long e-mail!

Karen: I know, isn't it great! So while we're wrapping up collaboration, what are your final thoughts?

Josh: I don't really know.

Karen: Well, what happens when you and Tim collaborate?

Josh: Well, he has an idea, and then I have an idea. He usually has really different ideas than mine, and sometimes that's really frustrating. Other times it's really interesting.

Karen: That sounds a lot like what Stacy was saying in her e-mail about collaboration. When people bring all their different ideas it can make something much better than if it was just your idea.

Josh: Oh yes . . . that's right . . . I didn't realize that!!

Despite this ah-ha moment, when we played cards later that night Josh was intent on winning, and grumpy when he lost. I wondered how this competitive child of mine would draw on the collaborative skills that are so important in developing good relationships in all aspects of life. Would certain things easily trigger his defensive behaviors? Would he be able to let go of winning? Would he know when to compromise and when to stand firm? I made a mental note to help him understand that winning is good in certain circumstances, but perhaps he didn't need to get so frustrated if he loses at cards once in a while!

> "When [collaboration] works it is 1+1 = 3 in terms of impact."
> Orla, Northern Ireland

As we got in the car the next morning to drive around the park, I realized that some of the conversations were having an impact. I wondered out loud how many of the animals we'd read about we might see, and Josh responded with enthusiasm. "OK Mom! You take the left side, I'll take the right side, and we'll look for wildlife. It'll be like being in a team."

I smiled. He was right; it was a team. My son and I had created this small team, for this long journey, and it was by far the best team I've ever joined.

Karen Davey-Winter

Complete the following sentences:

1. I am most collaborative when . . . ..

2. I am least collaborative when . . .

3. My defenses are triggered by . . .

4. The strengths that I bring to a team are . . .

5. To me, being collaborative means . . .

Josh's Journal

Week 7

August 2nd, 2012
Today I went to the Grand Canyon of the Yellowstone and West Thumb Geysers and went on a lake boat. Sweet!

August 3rd, 2012
Today I went white water rafting and horseback riding. Cool!

August 4th, 2012
Today went and saw the movie *Total Recall*. P.S. - Sweet!

August 5th, 2012
Today I went to an indoor waterpark. Cool! P.S. - It's Evan's Plunge!

August 6th, 2012
Today I went to Crazy Horse Memorial and Mount Rushmore. Fab!

August 7th, 2012
Today I saw the Badlands. First, great. Mid, OK. End, help!

August 8th, 2012
Today first I went to Sioux Falls. Also I went to Thunder Speedway. Last I went to an awesome pool. Sizzlin'.

Curiosity

Week 7: Sioux Falls, South Dakota, via Yellowstone National Park, Jackson and Casper, Wyoming.

Total mileage so far: 8,455.

Theme for Week 7: Curiosity.

> **"Curiosity is the very basis of education and if you tell me that curiosity killed the cat, I only say the cat died nobly."**[77]
> **– Arnold Edinborough**

Just before we turned out the lights on the last day of our sixth week, I told Josh that our theme for the next week would be *Curiosity*.

Josh: Oh, I don't think that's a very good idea.
Karen: Oh why's that?
Josh: Well, oh wait. We're doing the rafting and going to Mount Rushmore . . . OK, maybe it is a good idea!

For Josh, curiosity was about action and adventure. For me, it was about learning and exposure to new experiences. This whole trip was based in curiosity; it

> *"Curiosity is the engine that moves us forward as a species."*
> Antonio, California, USA

was an expedition and we were explorers. We were learning new things, creating new experiences, and building new connections. There were opportunities and possibilities. There was also uncertainty. For me, the uncertainty was in having given up work for eight weeks. For Josh, it was in not quite knowing what to expect each day. But curiosity got the better of us, and as Todd Kashdan says in his insightful book *Curious*, "Instead of trying desperately to explain and control our world, as a curious explorer we embrace uncertainty."[78]

Throughout the week I was reminded of The Choice Map,[79] from Marilee Adams' book *Change Your Questions, Change Your Life*. "In every instance of our lives we're faced with choosing between the Learner Path and the Judger Path."[80] If we choose the Learner Path, we are curious, and we want to learn more about people or circumstances. If we choose the Judger Path, we react with judgment, making assumptions about others or ourselves. Approaching life with a Learner mindset helps us build better relationships, leverage our experiences, and achieve better outcomes. When we approach life with a Judger mindset, we get stuck and back ourselves into a corner, and our relationships suffer. We all move from one to the other; the key is to know where we are and how to get back on the Learner Path. We can do that by changing the questions we ask ourselves. Instead of Judger questions like, "How can I prove that I'm right," or, "What's wrong with him," we ask Learner questions such as, "What am I contributing," or, "What might they be feeling?" Curiosity takes us from Judger to Learner.

The seventh week of the trip was more fun when we stayed in Learner mode. We saw opportunities to learn about National Parks. We expanded our horizons with activities like horseback riding and white water rafting. And we made connections with people and listened to their stories. When we became tired or frustrated, we moved into a Judger mindset. Our defenses went up, our vulnerabilities were triggered, and we stopped being able to see possibilities. Being in Judger constrained us. When we used our curiosity to challenge our reactions and explore different perspectives, we moved ourselves back on the Learner Path and our experiences were richer.

&

"A sense of curiosity is nature's original school of education"[81] – Smiley Blanton

Yellowstone National Park was America's first national park, established in 1872 and reaching into Wyoming, Montana and Idaho. Our visit had begun at Mammoth Hot Springs, with its spectacular rock formations and trickling hot water. As we drove to the lodge where we were staying, we passed geysers, elk, bison, mountains, lakes, canyons, and more hot springs. Every few minutes we saw something new. It was like opening a treasure chest. Our curiosity started to build.

We got up early on the first day of the seventh week, inspired by our arrival the day before and ready to make the most of the day. We left the hotel, armed with a wildlife identification guide provided by the hotel visitor center, a pen, and a map. Today would be an adventure, and we were all set. We started by driving to Artist's Point, where we hiked to the Grand Canyon of Yellowstone. It was breathtaking with its bright yellow rock, gushing waterfalls, and rainbows created when the sunlight passed through the water. We continued to hike around the North Rim, stopping at points along the way to get different perspectives and views. Josh's enthusiasm was palpable and increased as the day wore on. He checked off moose and elk on his wildlife-spotting sheet and focused on searching for other animals. As we drove through the park, he was delighted when we came upon some bison, sauntering calmly in the middle of the road, surrounded by traffic. He took hundreds of pictures with my phone. The enthusiasm generated by his curiosity was contagious.

Kashdan says, "When we are curious, we are open to expanding ourselves, and to do so we explore."[82] We continued

> "Curiosity is a baby discovering the world."
> Shirley, Virginia, USA

our adventure in the afternoon with a boat trip on Yellowstone Lake. While we were waiting for the boat, we pulled out the maps, park guides, and the wildlife identification game. We reviewed where we'd been. We actually read the national park guides, something we hadn't done very thoroughly elsewhere, and we learned about the animals. On the boat trip, we learned that in the winter Bison walk on the ice to reach the islands in the middle of the lake. We learned about the Continental Divide, in the middle of the Lake, where the water flows to the Atlantic on one side and the Pacific on the other.

"Children are born with boundless curiosity,"[83] Kashdan writes. Certainly it was easy to be curious in one of the most fascinating places in the world, but it was also clear that curiosity begets curiosity. As we learned more, our minds became more inquisitive and we asked more questions. We made connections between different pieces of information and applied them to our world. Our curiosity resulted in lively conversations with others, and we learned even more. Our perspectives expanded. The energy we generated was positive, and our connection to each other was enhanced. We had been on the Learner Path all day.

> **REFLECTION**: Reflect on the last time you were curious. What did it feel like? What made you open to the experience? How did it impact your relationships?

> **ACTION**: Identify an upcoming situation where you can recreate that feeling of curiosity. It could be something mundane or it could be something that you already expect to be exciting. How does focusing on being curious impact your experience? What did you learn?

You may complete this exercise and all the exercises in the chapter in the exercise section at the back of the book and share your observations on my blog at: http://worklifeperspectives.com/Life_is_a_Road_Trip_.html

✐

"The important thing is not to stop questioning. Curiosity has its own reason for existing." [84] **Albert Einstein**

Later that week we arrived in Hot Springs to visit Mount Rushmore National Memorial and Crazy Horse Memorial. As we set out

> *"Curiosity is a willingness to engage and learn."*
>
> Shirley, Virginia, USA

from the hotel, we were most curious about Mount Rushmore, the famous mountain carved with the faces of George Washington, Thomas Jefferson, Theodore Roosevelt, and Abraham Lincoln. We were excited to see what it looked like and our expectations were high. But we passed the Crazy Horse Memorial first, and decided to visit that before the main event. I was somewhat disappointed that we would have to wait until the afternoon to see Mount Rushmore. Neither of us had read much about the memorial, which was modeled on the Native American war leader of the Oglala Lakota tribe.

I couldn't have been more surprised. Firmly on the Learner Path, our curiosity increased as we watched the movie about the history of the memorial. We discovered that its mission was to honor Native American Indians and that the image of Crazy Horse was chosen because he was considered a great patriotic hero. Korczak Ziolkowski, a passionate supporter of American Indians, was selected as the sculptor, and he started work in 1948. The project became his life's work, and seven of his ten children are involved in the project today. The memorial foundation does not take government funds; it believes in individual enterprise and private initiatives, and it hopes that people who believe in the memorial's mission will support it. It remains unfinished.

In the afternoon, we carried on to Mount Rushmore. Despite having been so excited about visiting it, we were initially disappointed. It was smaller than the Crazy Horse Memorial, and we couldn't summon up the same good feelings we had as we had listened to the story of how a family had collaborated to build Crazy Horse. We started to go down the Judger Path. Why had the American government thought they had a right to build such a monument on Native American land? How presumptuous!

But we drew on our curiosity and investigated further. Both memorials make important statements and both have some amount of controversy associated with them. Some people believe there is a theme of racial superiority associated with Mount Rushmore; some people claim that creating Crazy Horse's image in the mountainside without permission from his ancestors goes against his spirit. Rarely are things as clear as they seem at first glance, and our curiosity allowed us to explore the complexity.

> **REFLECTION:** Think of a time when you thought you had a clear view of something and then were disappointed. What you expected was not true; there was ambiguity instead of clarity. How did it make you feel when you thought things were clear? How did it change when it became obvious that the situation was more complex?

> **ACTION:** The next time you find yourself in a situation that seems to be clear, ask yourself a different set of questions to gain a new perspective. Be curious.

What happens? What new insights do you gain about yourself, others and the situation?

෴

"Let go of certainty. The opposite isn't uncertainty. It's openness, curiosity and a willingness to embrace paradox."[85] **– Tony Schwartz**

After we left Yellowstone National Park, we drove to Jackson, ninety miles south of the park entrance. We were scheduled for a day of

> *"Curiosity is letting go of ego and arrogance and knowing."*
>
> Shirley, Virginia, USA

adventure, starting with a white water rafting trip on the Snake River. The forty miles of the Teton mountain range surrounded us. The sun was hot, sparkling as it shone on the side of the mountains. The water was cold, rushing rapidly in parts of the river and winding slowly elsewhere. In a break between rapids, our guide told us that we could swim in the river. Josh, the youngest on our boat, could hardly wait to get in the water. As he jumped off the side he shouted, "Come on, Mom, it will be great." As he landed in the water, his face looked shocked from the cold.

Josh: Come on, Mom. Seriously, it's not that cold.
Karen: Right! I could see that look of horror on your face. There's absolutely no chance that I'm coming in!
Josh: Honestly, it's fine when you get in. It's almost warm even.
Karen: Then why are you shivering?
Josh: It's just a reaction. Come on, it's fun.

There was no way I was diving in. I knew how cold the water was from the rapids that had showered us earlier. Just as curiosity had motivated Josh to get in and experience the cold, assumptions caused my resistance. My curiosity had disappeared. I knew what to expect, I knew I would be cold and miserable, and I didn't want to experience it. I was just fine where I was, sitting on the edge of the boat, watching the joy that my son was experiencing.

But what if I had chosen to join him? What if I had let go of what I knew, of my assumptions, of my certainty? I didn't go in, so I can't be sure, but I suspect that my connection with him would have been enhanced. My choice would have had a different consequence. We would have shared another experience and gained something else to talk and laugh about, another memory to look back on.

ACTION: The next time you find yourself resisting trying something new, stop. Draw on your curiosity, let go of your assumptions, and make a different choice.

REFLECTION: How did it feel? What did you learn about yourself? What can you let go of in future? How does this impact you?

❦

"Getting to know someone else involves curiosity about where have they come from, who they are."[86] **– Penelope Lively**

As the week went by, we started to notice the relationship between curiosity and connection. When we arrived in our motel in Sioux Falls, we were surprised to find that the building was old and drab, without the familiar bright signage of most motels across the country. It was about a mile from downtown next to a hospital. We walked up to our room through long corridors with brown décor, and we felt like we were at school. The rooms, on the other hand, were huge, and more importantly offered the TV channels Josh needed to watch the Olympics. I wondered whether there was a story behind the odd location of the hotel. I started to go online to investigate, and then I stopped myself. Instead of going online, deducing, or making assumptions, I realized I could ask. If I asked, I might learn more, and I might make a connection.

The next day, I asked the person at the front desk to tell me about the motel. I felt some initial cautiousness – perhaps she thought I was being nosy?

"I try to be curious about the people I meet, find out who they are and what makes them interesting."
Antonio, California, USA

93

But she responded with warmth and explained that the hospital treated people with long-term illnesses. Patients often came from out of town for days or weeks, and the hotel was established to serve them. That led to questions and conversation about how long she had worked there, the mission of the hospital, and the trip we were on. We created a connection out of an everyday conversation, and it was curiosity that drove us. As Kashdan says, "Curious people act in certain ways with strangers that allow relationships to develop more easily."[87]

ACTION: Identify one of the following situations in which to be more curious.
- When you meet someone new
- With someone you don't know very well

Ask questions to understand more about who they are and what is important to them. Share some information about yourself. Listen.

REFLECTION: How did being curious and listening affect your connection with them? Did you identify any resistance or anxiety in yourself about using your curiosity this way? What did you learn about yourself?

❧

"Searching and exploring requires attention, awareness and effort."[88] – Todd Kashdan

As we sat in the hotel one evening in Sioux Falls, Josh decided to start researching roller coasters. It's one of his favorite pastimes. He can quote the make, year built, drop angle, speed, number of cars, and duration of the ride for most of the coasters he has ridden. He even knows some of that information for rides he plans to go on in the future. As he was watching clips about top amusement parks on YouTube, he realized there was a Six Flags amusement park in Chicago, Illinois. We were headed to Chicago the following week.

Josh: Mom, can we go? Pleeease?

Karen: Another Six Flags? Really? We've already been to two of them. We're going to Cedar Point in just over a week anyway, and that will have much better rides.

Josh: But Mom, it's my favorite thing to do. You know that.

Karen: Yes, I do. But how different can each Six Flags park be?

Josh: Look, this one has some really different rides.

Karen: I don't know, we'll see. If we can't print tickets out in advance at the next hotel, then it will cost a fortune, so probably not.

But he began quoting information about the various rides anyway. He begged me to come and look at the YouTube clips, convinced this would make me see reason

> *"Being overloaded gets in the way. If one has no time or energy or bandwidth, there is no opportunity to indulge curiosity., Perhaps curiosity necessarily requires time"*
>
> *Orla, Northern Ireland*

and trigger my curiosity. I responded with irritation. I was simply exhausted by the thought of it. He was disappointed.

Kashdan says, "Practicing curiosity can be difficult."[89] At the gym the next morning, I thought more about the amusement park conversation. I felt I had dampened Josh's enthusiasm and discouraged his curiosity. Did I want to give him the message that I was too tired to listen to the things that were important to him? Even if we couldn't get advance tickets, I could have shared his excitement about the rides – something I'd done many times before. I had the chance to learn more about what makes him tick, and I ignored it. I had an opportunity to practice curiosity. I'd thrown it away, and I felt terrible.

"We need energy to act on our curiosity, and we need curiosity to discover what works to replenish our energy,"[90] Kashdan writes. I decided to use my curiosity to determine how I could increase my energy. I finished my workout, adding some extra time because exercise energizes me. I got back to the room and gazed at my wonderful sleeping child, feeling so grateful that he's in my life. I knew that reminding myself of that gratitude helps bring life into focus. I drew on the empathy I had practiced earlier in the trip, and I imagined how it had felt for Josh when I had responded to his enthusiasm with irritation. I could almost physically feel his disappointment.

The next hotel had a printer, and I ordered the cheaper advance tickets for Six Flags. As we got in the car, Josh said, "I know you were busy and tired the other night. But now that we have the tickets, can I show you some of the rides on

> *"If I take a moment to be empathetic, I am first curious, 'What he could be thinking?'"*
> Ann, California, USA

YouTube tonight?" I apologized for not being engaged the other day and decided that this time I would be curious.

When we arrived at the hotel later, we sat down at the computer for most of the evening, comparing the rides, looking at the park map, and deciding our strategy for getting around the park. With my renewed curiosity, I realized afresh how analytical Josh is and how he has a great memory for details. I could see him drawing conclusions from information and conducting a comparative analysis. He was so excited and so curious. For me, practicing curiosity with something I had done many times before allowed me to see him from a new perspective.

REFLECTION: Think of an activity that you have to do so regularly that it has become mundane. The next time you do this activity, re-energize your curiosity. Search for something new in the activity, look for a different perspective. Make notes on your reflection.

ACTION: Talk to someone else about your experience. What new things did you notice? What did you learn about yourself? How did actively practicing curiosity change your experience?

❧

"Never judge a man's actions until you know his motives."[91]
– Anonymous

There was one moment during this week when I found myself firmly in a Judger mindset, struggling to draw on my curiosity. We were horseback riding in Jackson, Wyoming, after completing our white water rafting trip in the morning. When we arrived, they couldn't find our reservation. I sighed with irritation as the assistant looked ineffectually for our booking, and my empathy and curiosity were nowhere to be found. After about ten minutes we were assigned to a guide, and we got on our horses. Josh was excited. His horse was huge and lively; my horse sounded like she was crying and unhappy to start the trail.

As we started out, the guide told us my horse hated being separated from her mate, and he had been needed for a larger party. Toward the end of our ride, as we headed back to the stables, the larger party was making its way toward us. My horse suddenly made a loud neighing sound, turned around, and charged toward the group. She had seen her mate and was not willing to let him go by without trying to join him. I was terrified. The ground seemed a long way down, and I have no real idea how to ride a horse. My horse was strong, too, ignoring my frantic tugging on the reins. I was going to lose control, and I thought I would look incompetent or get hurt.

The Achilles heel I had battled earlier in the trip reappeared, and I took myself further down the Judger Path by asking Judger questions. Why on earth didn't they keep the two horses together if they knew they didn't like to be apart? Why was this guide not taking control of the situation? Why was I crazy enough to sign us up for this? As Kashdan says, "We get so focused on not looking like idiots that we get trapped inside our heads talking to ourselves."[92]

> "I think the more curious you are about the things you don't know, the less judgmental you are going to be."
>
> Antonio, California, USA

In only a few moments I had gone all the way down the Judger path. And then I realized. I had some choices. I could stay on the Judger Path, in an attempt to avoid the vulnerable feeling that comes with looking stupid, or I could approach this with curiosity. I tried to think of a question to take me back to the Learner Path. What information was I missing in this situation? Since I knew very little about horses, there was potentially a wealth of information that I didn't have. What else might be going on here? What skills does the guide have that I don't have? How can I encourage him to use those skills so that my horse doesn't throw me off?

Adams calls curiosity "the fast track to Learner."[93] With some effort I pulled myself back onto the Learner Path. As the guide tried to calm my horse, I took a breath. I asked him what I could do to help, and he gave me some instructions on how to handle the reins. I found out that they rarely let the two horses go on the same trail because they are much more difficult to control together. We were only on the trail at the same time as the larger group because of the error in our reservation; typically the two horses were only close to each other in the stable. Asking questions allowed me to see a different perspective. The guide clearly did know what he was doing. My assessment of his competence was wrong, just as my judgment of myself as looking foolish was unnecessary. As Adams says, "Every single one of us has Judger moments . . . it's a natural part of being human"[94]

ACTION: The next time you find yourself going down the Judger path, walk yourself through the ABCC process that Adams outlines in *Change Your Questions Change Your Life*:[95]

A – Aware - Am I in Judger?
B – Breathe – Do I need to step back, pause, and look at this situation more objectively?
C – Curiosity – Do I have all the facts? What is happening here?
C – Choice – What's my choice?

REFLECTION: How did going through the above affect the outcome? What did you learn about yourself?

"Curiosity is the engine of growth,"[96] Kashdan says, and we had grown a lot in this week. Visiting so many fascinating places while focusing on curiosity had given us more information,

> *"Those people who retain an interest in the world seem to have a far happier, healthier and vastly more interesting old age than those who retreat to the sofa (Olympics excepted!)"*
> *Alex, England*

understanding, and perspective. We had learned that holding onto curiosity in the face of assumptions and anxiety allowed us to navigate situations in a more positive way. And that enhanced our connection to each other and to others. Just as with the other themes, we found that practicing curiosity with intention was essential when tiredness, defensiveness, and vulnerability got in the way. And we had seen ourselves go down the Judger Path. Triggers we had learned about earlier in our journey had shown up again, we'd recognized them, and we had found a way to move beyond them.

We also made a deal after our visit to Crazy Horse Memorial. We agreed that Josh would bring me back for my seventieth birthday. We would be able to see the progress on the memorial, relive the memories, and explore something new. Our curiosity drove us to make that deal, and I knew it would drive us to keep it. Because, as Kashdan says, "What is the ingredient to creating a fulfilling life? The answer is curiosity."[97]

Complete the following sentences:

1. I am most curious when I ....

2. I am most judgmental when I ....

3. Uncertainty and ambiguity make me feel ....

4. The thing that stops me being curious is ....

5. The benefit of being curious is ....

Josh's Journal

Week 8

August 9th, 2012
Today I went to Mall of America and it was huge!

August 10th, 2012
Today I went to Bay Beach Amusement Park and played mini golf. Nice!

August 11th, 2012
Today I went to Lambeau Field. It was cool!

August 12th, 2012
Today I went to Tundra Lodge Water Park. Sweet!

August 13th, 2012
Today I went to The Field Museum and to a Cubs game. Great!

August 14th, 2012
Today I went to Six Flags Great America and had a blast. Amazing!

August 15th, 2012
Today I went up in Willis Tower. Amazing!

August 16th, 2012
Today I went to Cedar Point. It had the most awesome coasters. Best day ever!

Gratitude

Week 8: Home (Kensington, Maryland); via Minneapolis, Minnesota; Green Bay, Wisconsin; Chicago, Illinois; and Sandusky, Ohio.

Total mileage: 9,898.

Theme for Week 8: Gratitude.

"If the only prayer you ever say in your entire life is thank you, it will be enough."[98] **- Meister Eckhart**

With the exception of Freedom and Gratitude, I had assigned all of our weekly themes in random order. I had not given any thought

> *"How fitting to end the book with gratitude."*
>
> Orla, Northern Ireland

to the timing or tried to coordinate them with our activities and visits; they were simply themes that felt important in living a rewarding life. However, I deliberately chose to focus on gratitude for the last week. I knew that by the end of the trip I would be feeling grateful for having taken this time out of my everyday life to experience something new, and I was right. And as we drove toward Minneapolis, Josh and I discussed the last theme.

Karen: Tomorrow we will have a new theme – we'll be at the end of curiosity.
Josh: What's the last one going to be?
Karen: Gratitude.
Josh: What's gratitude?
Karen: Being thankful for what we have.
Josh: Ah. Well, I'm thankful for my life, and I'm thankful for you.
Karen: Oh thank you, I'm so grateful for you too!

It's difficult to describe the gratitude I felt after that conversation and as I reflected on the previous seven weeks. I was grateful to have a job that allowed me to take time off. I was grateful that I could afford the trip. I was grateful for the new experiences we'd had and the chance to reconnect with friends and places. I was grateful for the chance to look at life through a different lens each week and for the lessons I had learned. I was grateful for our adventures and for the time that I had spent with my son. It was the longest number of consecutive hours that I had spent with him in his lifetime. Nothing could compare with that.

In *Attitudes of Gratitude*, M. J. Ryan writes, "Wherever you choose to notice the goodness in your life, you will experience the uplift of gratefulness."[99] Earlier in the year I had read some books about happiness, and I knew that a significant way of increasing happiness was by changing your attitude and practicing gratitude. As we started this last week, I felt sad that the trip was coming to an end. This amazing trip,

> *"I live in a place of gratitude and make a daily point to gladly give thanks for everything that is around me."*
>
> Antonio, California, USA

so long in the making, would soon be over. And I knew that paying attention to gratitude would turn that sadness into sweet sorrow. As the week went by, I experienced a peacefulness that stayed with me long after we arrived home.

ঔ

"It is not joy that makes us grateful; it is gratitude that makes us joyful."[100] David Steindl-Rast

As we drove toward Minneapolis, Josh was excited about visiting the Mall of America. This is the largest mall in the country, with more than 520 stores and 40 million visitors each year. It is the size of seven football stadiums. Much more importantly to Josh, it has an amusement park with roller coasters, mini golf, and an aquarium. I braced myself for another afternoon of rides. We

> *"You can make all the difference in the world to someone by being certain to express your gratitude."*
>
> Stacy, Virginia, USA

planned to spend three days of this last week in amusement parks, and Josh would be in heaven.

As we pulled into the mall, I reminded Josh again that our theme was gratitude. His response was, "What's that again? The early themes were easy. The last few have been long words and really hard!" I assumed that all I had to do was ask him what he was grateful for, and he would answer with clear examples. I thought that by focusing on gratitude in that way, presto, we would be happier. But it didn't exactly work that way. I initially tried to get him to write about gratitude in his journal.

> **Karen**: So, since we're looking for gratitude this week, I'm thinking perhaps as well as writing one interesting thing you've done every day in your journal, you can also add one thing you're grateful for.
> **Josh [looking horrified]:** But I can't start that now, it wouldn't make sense. I haven't been doing it for the other weeks.
> **Karen**: Hmm . . . OK, but I'm going to journal things I'm grateful for. So I want you to share with me at least one thing you're grateful for from each day, and I'll ask you about it over dinner, OK? Doesn't have to be a big thing, just something from that day.
> **Josh**: OK.

Despite spending a large part of the week in amusement parks, which would normally inspire gratitude and happiness, it was challenging for him to be specific when I asked him what he was grateful for. We had a number of conversations, like the following, that exemplified his struggle.

> **Karen**: So, what is the one thing you're grateful for today?
> **Josh**: Being awesome.
> **Karen**: Ah . . . and what specifically today are you grateful for?
> **Josh**: Being awesome.
> **Karen [detecting he's not taking this seriously]:** But do you have anything specific?
> **Josh**: I don't know! This is too hard!

Or this:

> **Karen**: So, what is the one thing you're grateful for today?
> **Josh**: My life.

Karen: Ah . . . and what specifically about your life are you grateful for?
Josh: Just my life.
Karen [giving up]: Ah.

I was frustrated. My questions seemed to have no effect. But later I realized that the discussion of gratitude was having an influence. He was showing gratitude, just not when I asked him or in the way I expected. I just had to pay closer attention. When I did, I noticed the following:

- After purchasing some new sneakers at the Mall of America, he touched my arm and said, "Thanks for buying these sneakers at the best mall in the world!"
- Over dinner at the Grand Lux Café in Chicago, in the middle of a dessert that involved four chocolate cupcakes, three different frostings, and five different toppings, he paused to say, "Thanks for taking me to Six Flags and for this awesome trip."
- As we drove away from the stadium where the Green Bay Packers play, he said, "Thanks for taking me to Lambeau Field, Mom."
- As we took our last ride at Cedar Point, he hugged me and said, "Thanks for taking me to the best amusement park in the world!!"

He was showing gratitude, but his choice was to verbalize it as he felt it, not write it down or recite it at a prearranged time. "Developing the muscle of gratitude is just like exercising any other," Ryan says, adding that a daily ritual to help it develop can take many forms. "Only you know what will work best for you."[101]

"When you focus on gratitude, and consider all of the blessings in your life, not only does your gratitude grow, but so does your joy, and your happiness, and the positivity in your life."
Christina, Virginia, USA

ACTION: For the next week, practice gratitude at least once a day. Try a different approach each time. Complete a journal entry, write a note in your phone, call a friend, and send an email. Identify a way of recording gratitude that is most comfortable for you.

REFLECTION: What did you learn? What felt most comfortable and authentic? What do you think would happen if you practiced gratitude in that way for a week?

You may complete this exercise and all the exercises in the chapter in the exercise section at the back of the book and share your observations on my blog at: http://worklifeperspectives.com/Life_is_a_Road_Trip_.html

So what was my way of practicing gratitude? Every day I noted in my journal at least three things I was grateful for. Some days it was the big things – my son, my health, my family and friends. Other days it was the incidental things that happened during the day – the way someone helped me at the mall, the hot tub at the Green Bay hotel that helped me sleep better, the fact that roller coasters don't fall apart despite great speeds and heights.

In her insightful book *The How of Happiness*, Sonja Lyubomirsky says, "The expression of gratitude is a kind of metastrategy for achieving happiness."[102] Being mindful of gratitude meant that I saw it in our activities throughout the week. When we visited Lambeau Field, home of the Green Bay Packers, I watched in wonder as Josh interacted with our guide. He laughed and joked, he was interested in the stories the guide told, and he was fascinated by the information being imparted. As we walked toward the tunnel that the players take to get to the field, the guide asked Josh if he'd like to join him. They walked together at the front of the group as if they were leading the players onto the field for a match. I was grateful in that moment for Josh's lively personality, his confidence, and his ability to make almost everything he does fun. As I focused on my gratitude, I felt happy.

By the time we reached Chicago, we only had one more stop on our itinerary, only one more hotel to check into, and only four days left before heading home. Over dinner in Chicago one evening, after visiting the second of three amusement parks for the week, we discussed our trip and how little time we had left. We remembered some of our adventures, the activities that were most fun, and the people we'd stayed with. At one point, Josh started making fun of my accent and the way that I pronounce

> *"It is not essential to be grateful to be happy, but maybe it is essential to feel gratitude in order to be happy in the long run."*
>
> *Orla, Northern Ireland*

"banana." He was exaggerating a British accent to make a point. We laughed, and I told him I was grateful for being able to laugh with him. Counting our blessings and being thankful for our experiences not only increased our happiness, but it also increased our connection. As Martin Seligman says in his recent book *Flourish*, "When we express our gratitude to others, we strengthen our relationship with them."[103]

ACTION: Using the method of practicing gratitude that you identified in the previous exercise, practice gratitude for a week. In particular, focus on areas of your life or relationships that you want to improve.

REFLECTION: What happened? How did practicing gratitude affect your sense of happiness and well-being? How did it impact your relationships with others?

❧

"It's good to have an end to journey toward; but it's the journey that matters in the end." [104] **- Ursula K Le Guin**

When I had planned the trip earlier in the year, I expected that I would be exhausted from driving by the last week, so I had booked the hotel in Green Bay for three nights. Our average stay in any single place was two nights – sometimes a night or two longer when we stayed with friends. Often we only stayed one night before moving on, so three nights felt like a luxury. I had never been to Green Bay, but it has a National Football League (NFL) team, so I thought it would be a decent size and have a lot to do.

> *"Being grateful is honoring what is in your life your health, your partner, your job, your friends, your love and passion for what you do, your dreams, etc."*
>
> *Antonio, California, USA*

Sometimes it's difficult to remember to look for gratitude in discouraging situations. As we drove around that first evening, I felt puzzled. Where was the center of town? We found a local park with mini golf and go-karts. Then we saw a street with a couple of restaurants. The city wasn't what I expected. I sent a friend of mine a text message, knowing that she had family in Wisconsin.

She replied, "Yes, it's really a small town. You'd think it would be bigger given it has an NFL team." I described where we were, and she replied, "That's right, you're in downtown. Enjoy!"

We visited the mini golf park three times. We took the tour of Lambeau Field and visited the Green Bay Packers Hall of Fame. Those activities only got us through lunchtime on the second day, and we had a day and a half left. What to do? I started to feel irritated. I told myself that I should have booked an extra night in Minneapolis or Chicago, and I should have researched the area in more detail. We were not making good use of our time.

And then I realized that instead of getting irritated, I had another choice. I could look at this from a place of gratitude. Instead of wishing I had done something differently, I could notice what was right about this moment. What could I be grateful for? I could be grateful for having the time to relax. I could be grateful for the pool in our hotel, which meant we had something fun to do every evening. I could be grateful for the time to sit and read a book while Josh watched the closing ceremony of the Olympics. I could be grateful for the opportunity to just be in the present moment. As Ryan says, "[Gratitude] helps us return to our natural state of joyfulness where we notice what's right instead of what's wrong."[105]

> "You have to choose to look at the good."
>
> Ann, California, USA

ACTION: The next time you find yourself frustrated with a situation, pause and reflect. Ask yourself, "What's right about this?" and, "What can I be grateful for?"

REFLECTION: What do you notice? How does choosing to look at a potentially negative situation in this way affect you?

"It would be wonderful if we didn't need the sorrows of other people to remind us of the blessings in our own lives." [106] **- M. J. Ryan**

Paying attention to gratitude also allowed me to experience it without being prompted by someone else's misfortune. However, there were a couple of times during the week when we saw or heard of another person's tragedy, and gratitude washed over me. I didn't need to be mindful to feel gratitude in those circumstances – in those situations my gratitude was a reflex.

At the start of the week, I got a call from a colleague at work. She had the terrible news that the husband of a

> *"Sometimes, some terrible thing happens, like Sandy Hook or 9/11, and you are forced to look at how lucky you are in comparison to others' misfortune. It is then a feeling of gratitude comes over you."*
>
> *Ann, California, USA*

work friend had died unexpectedly at the age of forty-six. I felt awful for her. I tried to imagine what she was going through, revisiting the theme of empathy from earlier in the trip. I told Josh about it, and he started talking about how her children might be feeling. He role-played a dialogue between the kids and their friends, trying hard to put himself in their shoes. That night I wrote in my journal about my friend, noting everything I was grateful for, large and small. Most especially I was grateful that neither I, nor anyone in my family, had suffered a tragedy that day.

Later in the week, we were leaving a restaurant in Green Bay to get into our car and return to the hotel. As we walked through the parking lot, we saw a man without legs on a skateboard, pushing himself around. My heart sank, and my reflexive thought was, "Oh gosh, I'm so lucky."

ACTION: The next time you hear of someone else's tragedy, take a moment to count your blessings. Notice your reaction – how reflexive is it to be grateful in that moment? Did you have to remind yourself to be grateful?

REFLECTION: Reflect on how being grateful affects your happiness levels that day and for the next few days. How would practicing gratitude, even when you are not comparing yourself to someone else's misfortune, impact your life? Try it.

❦

"Feeling gratitude and not practicing it is like wrapping a present and not giving it."[107] - William Arthur Ward

My car shows me it needs servicing with an oil-life indicator on the dashboard. At 15 percent, it's time to get the car serviced. I had anticipated needing to get it serviced in Portland, but the indicator still showed 50 percent there. I expected it again in Seattle, but it had only dropped to 40 percent. By the time we reached Minneapolis it was at 30 percent, but my fear of breaking down on the last leg of the journey overcame me, and I decided to get it serviced anyway. When I get my car serviced at home, I arrive when they open at 7:30 a.m., and I expect to wait a couple of hours and spend more than a hundred dollars. They always do a great job, I'm never dissatisfied, and I just know what to expect. So we got up early to get to the garage in Minneapolis. I assumed it would take the usual two hours. Based on that, I calculated when we'd arrive in Green Bay that evening and settled down with a cup of coffee and a book. Josh played on his iTouch and had his Kindle as a backup.

> *"Some people believe that gratitude that is not expressed is not gratitude at all."*
>
> Stacy, Virginia, USA

Within 30 minutes I heard my name being called. I assumed they had a question and had a minor panic that they'd found a problem. But they had finished. We scrambled to gather our belongings and went to check out. The person at the checkout said I owed $39.95. I was pleasantly surprised. I questioned the cashier, but she was sure it was done, and she was sure it only cost $39.95. I turned around and saw my car being driven out of the workshop and into the service bay.

> *"I actually think that making sure you show your gratitude often is not mostly for other people (although it does make them feel great); it is mostly for you. It keeps you focused on the good things in your life and helps you to have more joy in your heart. It helps you to be more kind to others."*
>
> Stacy, Virginia, USA

As Ryan says, "Attitudes are the underpinnings of action"[108] Does it count if you feel grateful and you don't act on it? I was tempted to quickly pay, get in the car, and get on the road. We could arrive in Green Bay ninety minutes earlier than planned. Perhaps we could find somewhere extra to stop on the way. However, if I rushed away, they wouldn't know how grateful I was.

> **Karen**: Thank you SO much. I can't believe how quickly that was finished. It normally easily takes two hours at home.
> **Cashier**: Where in Maryland are you from? Near Washington, D.C.?
> **Karen**: Kensington, which is about a thirty-minute drive to the White House if there is no traffic, although that's rare in the D.C. area! We've been driving around the country this summer, over eight thousand miles so far, so as you can imagine it's a relief to get the car serviced without problems!
> **Josh**: Yes, and we've visited two Six Flags amusement parks so far, plus some other smaller ones, and we're going to Six Flags in Chicago, too, AND Cedar Point amusement park!
> **Cashier**: Wow, that's quite the trip!!

I turned around and saw the mechanic walking towards us, and said, "Thank you so much for servicing our car so quickly – I really appreciate it. This experience has been so efficient!" He looked surprised – apparently not many people thank him for the work that he does.

We did arrive in Green Bay earlier than anticipated, although not by ninety minutes. However, taking that extra ten minutes to say thank you illuminated the relationship between gratitude, impact, and connection. Our gratitude had a positive impact; that impact had created a connection. All of us left the exchange smiling.

> **REFLECTION**: How often do you find yourself feeling grateful but not expressing it or acting on it? What situations hold you back?

> **ACTION**: The next time you're feeling grateful, express it. Explain why, don't just say thank you. Use the opportunity to build a connection. What is the impact on both you and the others involved?

〰

"The hardest arithmetic to master is that which enables us to count our blessings."[109] **- Eric Hoffer**

So what gets in the way of gratitude? During this last week, there were a few moments when my thoughts turned to going back to work. I needed to buy liability insurance, and I needed to check in to confirm that all my paperwork was signed. I left a couple of messages for the director who manages my client's account, asking him to call me back so that we could confirm everything. I didn't hear back from him for a day or so, but I didn't think too much of it. Then I got a voicemail back from him saying, "We need to talk."

When someone tells me, "We need to talk," I usually assume that means bad news is coming. I couldn't recall a time when I'd heard those words and I'd enjoyed the rest of the conversation. So I went down a negative spiral of worry, and the monologue in my head went something like this:

- *Oh no, it's never good when someone says, "We need to talk."*
- *Perhaps my contract has been terminated because I've been away for so long.*
- *But surely not, everyone seemed fine about me leaving. I've heard from a couple of people through the trip, nothing major seems to have happened.*
- *But eight weeks is a long time, all kinds of things of things could have changed.*
- *Perhaps no one wanted to ruin my trip, so they're waiting until I get back to tell me.*
- *OK, what's the worst that could happen? I have enough money to last for a while – I'm sure I could find a new contract relatively quickly.*
- *But there are a lot of things to buy right before Josh goes back to school.*

And I went on and on. All thoughts of gratitude flew from my mind. When

> *"Gratitude brings peace and contentment and helps prolong these feelings."*
>
> Orla, Northern Ireland

I am in that state of worry, it is almost impossible to move myself back to a place of gratitude.

Ryan says, "One of the incredible truths about gratitude is that it is impossible to feel both the positive emotion of thankfulness and a negative emotion such as anger and fear at the same time"[110] There is research that shows gratitude engages a specific area of the brain. When that part of the brain is activated, it cannot easily engage in both positive and negative stimuli.[111] I took a breath. I focused on today and what I was grateful for in that moment. I was grateful that it was supposed to be sunny for our day at Cedar Point. I was grateful that the car was in good shape after its service. I was grateful that my son and I were healthy.

Slowly, I started to feel calmer and more positive. I decided to use the phrase, "We need to talk," as an early warning system in the future, a sign that I would need to monitor my reactions. I was grateful that I could find a use for something that had initially sent me to a negative place. Even though it had taken some intentional effort, focusing on gratitude had pulled me out of my state of worry and back into the present. As Lyubomirsky says, "Gratitude is an antidote to negative emotions, a neutralizer of envy, avarice, hostility, worry and irritation."[112]

When I did finally speak to the account director, it turned out to be nothing. He was just busy catching up after being on vacation and hadn't gotten around to calling me back. It reminded me not to jump to conclusions and to wait until I had all the information before reacting in future. There are so often multiple explanations for a situation. And it's rarely the case that my initial interpretations, ones driven by my own fears, are the right ones!

> **REFLECTION:** What gets in the way of gratitude for you? Is it worry, self-judgment, fear, jealousy? Consider why this might be.

> **ACTION:** The next time you experience the feelings you have identified, pull yourself back into the present and count your blessings. How hard is it to do? What is the impact?

We spent the last day of our trip at Cedar Point. Of all the things we had seen and experienced, Josh was most excited about this day. I was grateful that we had something so exciting to do on the

> *"Funny but the word gratitude has the color blue to it, maybe because I see it as big and beautiful as the skies above us"*
>
> Antonio, California, USA

last day, which might otherwise have been anticlimactic. It was fantastic. We arrived early at Josh's suggestion, not mine, which was surprising, because I'm early for everything. He wanted to be waiting at the barrier when the park opened so that we could do a couple of the big rides before the lines became excruciatingly long. He had the right idea, too. We rode on two of the more popular coasters, the Millennium Force and Mantis, within forty-five minutes of our arrival. Josh was nearly skipping with delight. We rated the thrill factor of each ride we went on, assigning marks out of ten. We walked back and forth throughout the park, probably in excess of six miles. We strategized about the order in which we would ride so that we minimized the wait times. It took all day before I agreed to go on the Top Thrill Dragster (405 feet high, 120 miles per hour, and only a lap bar and belt to hold us in), but finally I did. It's hard to describe the gratitude I felt when the ride was over and we were still in one piece.

As we got in the car at about ten p.m. that night, Josh turned around to look at me from the passenger seat.

Josh: Thank you, Mom, for organizing the best trip ever. I want you to take three hundred dollars out of my bank account for the trip.
Karen: Oh Josh, you're so welcome, but I don't need you to pay any money toward it.
Josh [really upset]: No! I WANT to. I want you to take my three hundred dollars.
Karen: OK, thank you. I'll tell you what, if I need that three

> *"I am grateful to have a friend like you who asks me to think about these interesting things!"*
>
> Ann, California, USA

hundred dollars, I will know that it's there and I will know I can take it. And if I don't need it, you can keep it and we'll put it toward a car when you're older. How does that sound?
Josh: OK, that sounds good. Thank you, Mom.

I drove back to the hotel that night with joy in my heart. It was sad to know we were leaving the next morning. But just as I had anticipated at the start of the week, the gratitude that I felt turned that sadness into sweet sorrow.

Complete the following sentences:

1. I am thankful for ....

2. I most often feel gratitude when ....

3. The way that I most commonly practice gratitude is by ....

4. The thing that gets in the way of gratitude for me is...........................

5. I just need to ....in order to focus on the things that I'm thankful for.

Afterword

Reentry is difficult. As we pulled into our driveway in Kensington, it was hard to believe we were home. It felt awkward to be in our house, to not have to check into a hotel or to find our way around a new place. When we woke up the next morning, it felt strange to be able to make our own breakfast and to be free from packing a suitcase and loading it into the car. It was odd to be in one place, no longer constantly on the move. The trip of a lifetime was over, and readjusting to our everyday life would take a while.

We arrived home on a Friday. I went back to work the following Monday, and Josh had a week of camp before school started. When I dropped him off at camp, everything was pretty much as it had been when I'd picked up him the day before we left eight weeks before. There were some new kids and a few new pictures on the wall, but not much had changed. I arrived at work, sat down in my office, and started to work through my e-mail. A few projects had ended and some new ones had started, but nothing significant had changed. Initially people were excited to ask me about my trip, but it didn't take long before those conversations became few and far between. Life had carried on for everyone else. For Josh and me, our experiences stayed with us, hanging over our day-to-day activities, reminding us of everything we had learned.

About a month later, after school had started and it hardly felt like we had been away, I sat down with my notes from the trip. As I reread them, the trip came to life again. Memories revived as we talked about our varied adventures and the fun we had. I decided my process for writing the book would be as follows:

- I would aim to draft one chapter per month, and each chapter would focus on one theme.
- I would find a book or two related to the theme for the month and read them for reference.

- I would review my notes to look for subtopics and see how those aligned with the reference books that I had read.
- I would organize our experiences into the subtopics and then start writing.

Not surprisingly, each month I was reminded that when you pay attention to something, it shows up.

- When I was writing about freedom, I remembered that there were times when taking a different approach to life was more appropriate. For the most part, I went back to my schedules and to being organized, but I remembered that not everything in life requires that. When I stayed with friends in Florida during a weekend trip, I let go of the need to create a schedule and went with the flow. I became acutely aware of the people who allow me to truly be myself. I tried hard not to let my judgments of myself get in the way of being free to accept who I truly am.
- When I wrote about impact, I noticed the impact I had on others and what the impact of others told me about myself. A colleague at work was deliberating about whether to bring an issue to a senior leader, bypassing a couple of levels of management and potentially upsetting others in the process. I asked her what impact she wanted to have, and she paused, realizing that it might not be her best course of action. When I was affected by the sharp words of someone at work, I remembered to look at what my reaction was telling me about myself rather than trying to find explanations or blame in others. And I remembered that when I am short with people, it affects them negatively and is not the way I want to show up.
- When I was writing about kindness, I recalled how difficult it had been to show kindness to myself. When the logistics of life became more complicated after Josh joined a soccer team that practiced three times a week, thirty minutes away from home, I found myself getting frustrated and having to practice compassion for myself again. I remembered that showing kindness to others fills both my bucket and theirs, and I looked for opportunities to show kindness to people I didn't know.

- When I focused on connection, I looked for ways to stay connected during difficult conversations at home and at work. I reestablished connections with people I hadn't seen for a while. And I planned a trip back to Seattle to stay with Clare and Kaj, because my visit with them had reminded me of the importance of staying connected to the significant people in my life. It had also shown me the sense of belonging that connection brings.

- When I was writing about empathy, I remembered to look at situations from multiple perspectives before coming to a decision or choosing an approach. As a result, I had richer and more productive client meetings and an enhanced connection with Josh. I was delighted when Josh was selected to be a peer mediator at school. He explained that he needed to understand what was going on with people who were in conflict by putting himself in their shoes, and I knew our conversations about empathy had helped him.

- When I wrote about collaboration, I started noticing when people went into Green Zone and Red Zone behaviors at work. Discussions improved and decisions were more effective when I understood other people's interests. I helped a team navigate through conflict by reminding them to look at people's strengths and to leverage them. They understood each other better, and they worked more effectively as a team.

- Writing about curiosity reminded me to ask questions rather than make assumptions or jump to conclusions. I called on this a lot in my work and in my personal relationships. It meant I went down the Judger path less often, and that improved my conversations, relationships, and connections. I also liked myself more. Situations moved more quickly to a positive outcome than they might have otherwise.

- And finally, I remembered the power of gratitude and how being grateful blocks out negative feelings. When I found myself frustrated with something, I remembered to look for what was good in the situation. I regularly focused on how lucky I am to have my son, my friends, my family, and my work, and I found an increased sense of peace.

Just as reflecting on each theme during the trip resulted in increased awareness and more choices, so did focusing on a theme each month as I wrote the book. Mindfulness is powerful. The themes were relevant at home, at work, with Josh, and with my friends and family. I found ways to use what I had learned about the themes to try different strategies, and I noticed that I got different results. When I was writing about each theme, it seemed to show up everywhere, right at the forefront of my consciousness, guiding me to make different choices, have a different attitude, and make a different impact.

So, even though in the past I've made some of my biggest decisions on road trips, this trip wasn't about decisions. It was about reflecting, learning, and reaching a point of self-acceptance in my journey of life, my own road trip. It also contributed significantly to Josh's life journey, and only he will know what that meant for him and how it affects him as he continues on that journey.

It was with sweet sorrow that the road trip ended, but I anticipate it will be the start of a series of adventures. Before we started the trip, Josh's plan was that we would drive across the United States when he was ten, travel around Europe when he's thirteen, and travel around the world when he's eighteen. We already started Europe with a trip to Greece during Spring Break in 2013, and we've discussed a Mediterranean cruise for 2015. If he's still really interested in traveling around the world with me when he's eighteen, I will be shocked, but I will be right there with him.

CREATING YOUR OWN MINDFULNESS PROJECT

Anyone can live life in a more mindful, intentional way – you don't have to go on a road trip to do so! Here is a suggestion for taking the concepts described in this book and creating your own mindfulness project.

- Pick some themes that you're curious about, that you think will benefit you, or that someone has told you to pay attention to. They might be any of the themes in this book or they might be something else. Here are some additional suggestions:

  * Creativity
  * Ambiguity

* Expectations
* Respect
* Clarity
* Vulnerability
* Risk taking
* Belonging

- Once you have selected your themes, determine a timeframe to pay attention to each one. Will it be a day, a week, or a month? Will you pay attention to the theme at work, with your friends, when you're parenting, or all of the time? Keep in mind that once you start to pay attention to something in one aspect of your life, you will notice it everywhere.
- Create a set of questions for yourself about each theme so that you have a framework in which to focus. Your questions might include:

  * What does the theme mean to you? What does it look like, sound like, feel like?
  * What is the impact of the theme?
  * What gets in the way of the theme?
  * What would your world be like if there was more of the theme in it?
  * What happens to your relationships, your work, and how you show up when you pay attention to the theme?

- Decide whether you want to work on this mindfulness project with someone. It might be:

  * With a close friend, with both of you focusing on the same themes and sharing the results.
  * By soliciting input from other people to add more perspectives, such as posting the questions on Facebook or via e-mail to see what responses you get. Reflect on what new dimensions this gives you that you can learn from.

- Start your mindfulness project. Observe what happens. Keep a journal of the results if that's an effective activity for you. Reflect on what you learn about yourself, your reactions, your relationships, and how you show up.

I would love to hear your results! Please feel free to email me, or share via my blog at http://worklifeperspectives.com/Life_is_a_Road_Trip_.html. Enjoy the journey!

Acknowledgments

There are many people that made this book possible, and to whom I want to express my gratitude, especially:

- To everyone who replied to my weekly emails about the themes, providing me with insights and perspectives that often hadn't occurred to me, as well as providing a lively source of conversation with Josh. I used all of the insights provided, even if they don't appear as quotes in the book. Our experiences, and the lessons we learned, are richer because of them.
- To Elizabeth Gates, my writer's coach, who gave me extremely useful feedback (http://lonelyfurrowcompany.com). I have no doubt that the quality of my writing is significantly better than it would have been had I produced this book without her input.
- To Molly Johnstone-Clarke, my beautiful, smart niece, who designed the cover of the book. As the oldest of my nieces and nephews, my love for her was instrumental in my decision to have Josh on my own. And for that, as well as this book cover, I will always be immensely grateful.
- To Abby Srinivasan, who gave me copy-editing and thematic consistency input. She was the first person to print everything out like a book. In addition to giving me great feedback, she made it feel real for the first time.
- To Jill Gross, (jillsgross@gmail.com) for her attention to detail and for being the person to whom I could delegate when I could no longer see the spelling and grammatical mistakes. She copyedited the book but kept my voice, and in doing so she made me a better writer.
- To the others that read drafts of this book in various stages – Orla, Ann, Clare, Kaj, Jay, and Darren – whose feedback and encouragement kept me moving forward.

And, of course, the person to whom I am most grateful is my son, Joshua. As well as simply making the trip the best thing I've done in my life (besides having him), he constantly says or does things from which I can learn. He is smart, funny, independent, flexible, creative, fun-loving, and full of joy. I hope that the times he feels yelled at are significantly outweighed by the times he feels loved. Without him in my life, I would be less of a person; my life would be less rich. He is my favorite person in the world, and he would be even if he weren't my son.

Coaching Exercises

Freedom

The polarity map shows some of the complexity implicit in freedom, the choices we make, and the consequences of those choices. Moving around the polarity map changes the balance of the polar opposites, the balance between freedom and constraint. It also changes the consequences.

ACTION: Create a polarity map of your own. Choose a theme in your life – like freedom – that involves your biggest challenge or the thing that you most desire. Identify the polar opposites and enter them in the middle two boxes. Fill in the four squares with the upsides and downsides of each polarity. Locate yourself on the map and mark that place with an X.

REFLECTION: Reflect on where you are in the map. Is that where you want to be? If not, identify where you want to be with a Y on the map. How will you get there? What will the outcome of moving to Y be?

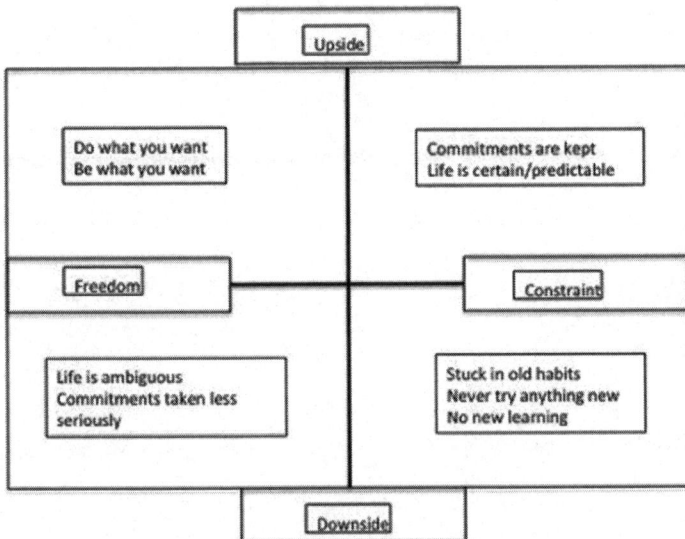

Upside	
Do what you want Be what you want	Commitments are kept Life is certain/predictable
Freedom	**Constraint**
Life is ambiguous Commitments taken less seriously	Stuck in old habits Never try anything new No new learning
Downside	

REFLECTION: What is your typical approach to life? Are you organized, flexible, spontaneous, structured? Think of some situations and identify the most consistent patterns for you.

ACTION: Choose a situation and identify the opposite approach. If you are normally structured, try being flexible. If you are normally organized, try being spontaneous. What happens? How does it feel? What did you learn about yourself?

REFLECTION: With whom and in what situation do you feel most free to be yourself? With whom and in what situation do you feel least able to be yourself? Why is that?

ACTION: Next time you are with the person that least enables you to be yourself, make a note of what happens. What do you notice about your relationship with that person? What did you learn about yourself?

REFLECTION: What situations cause the monologue in your head to go down a negative spiral of self-judgment? Why is that? What do you notice about your reactions?

ACTION: Next time you find yourself going down that negative spiral, stop. What is the worst that could happen? What could you do differently? Try changing your reaction. How does that affect the outcome? What did you learn about yourself?

REFLECTION: Identify a situation in which you are truly constrained by someone else. What is standing in the way of claiming your freedom? Next, identify a situation where you are putting undue constraint on another. What is causing you to put this constraint in place?

ACTION: Take action to stand up against those constraints. What happens? Now take action to remove the constraints you're putting on someone else. How does this impact your life? What do you learn about yourself?

Impact

ACTION: Choose a situation in which you feel safe to show vulnerability and try demonstrating it.

REFLECTION: What is the impact on others? What happens to the quality of your connection with that person?

ACTION: The next time you are solving a problem, notice your approach and notice the impact on people around you.

REFLECTION: What do you see and hear? Was the impact positive or negative? What did you learn about yourself?

REFLECTION: What tone do you use most often – encouraging, empathic, critiquing, shaming? Which approach makes you feel better and achieves the best result?

ACTION: The next time you make an observation to a co-worker, friend, or your children, think about the impact you want to have, and adjust your tone to line up with that. What was the result and what was the impact on them?

ACTION: The next time you feel yourself reacting to something someone says or does, pay close attention.

REFLECTION: What information does your reaction give you about yourself? What filters, biases, and lenses might be influencing your interpretation? How can you use this information to have a different impact in the future?

ACTION: Take a piece of paper and pen and imagine your signature on that piece of paper. Look at the paper and think about it for at least a minute. Visualize the flow of your writing, how the letters come together effortlessly. Then using the opposite hand than you normally write with, write your signature on the paper.

REFLECTION: To what extent does the signature look anything like the visual you had in your mind? Where else in your life are your intentions good, but the delivery falls short? How can you modify that? How could that modification change the impact that you have and change how you show up?

ACTION: The next time you react to something notice what assumptions you are making, and what judgments you make.

REFLECTION: Where do the judgments and assumptions come from? What does this tell you about the way that you interpret events in your life?

REFLECTION: What characteristic of yourself are you most afraid of people seeing? To what lengths do you go to in order to hide that from the world?

ACTION: Next time you feel are feeling vulnerable because of this, choose a different behavior. How does it feel? What was the result?

ACTION: Identify a situation or future event where you are worried that you will not be accepted by the group. Carefully plan a strategy for engaging, and think about how you want to impact other people.

REFLECTION: How did it feel to go through this process? What result did you want, and what result did you get?

Kindness

ACTION: For the rest of the day, approach every interaction that you have with kindness.

REFLECTION: What happens to the quality of your connection with the people that you interact with? How does it make you feel to approach life with kindness?

ACTION: Pick a moment to bestow a random act of kindness on someone you don't know.

REFLECTION: What was their reaction? How did that make you feel? What do you think the impact was on the person to whom you showed kindness?

REFLECTION: Reflect on the opportunities you have to be intentionally kind in a situation where you otherwise might not, such as a work situation where your colleagues expect you to behave in a certain way, the chaos of a crowded mall, or an encounter with an estranged friend or family member. Choose an opportunity where you know the other person will not be expecting kindness.

ACTION: Deliberately show up differently. Smile when you might have frowned; say thank you when you might not typically remember. Show kindness with intention. What happens?

REFLECTION: What is your Achilles'" heel when it comes to your ability to show kindness to yourself? What triggers this? What happens when it shows up?

ACTION: Next time you feel your Achilles' heel showing up, stop. Change your actions and choose to be more kind to yourself. What is the impact on yourself and those around you?

ACTION: Spend the next week being deliberately kind to yourself.

REFLECTION: How hard was it? How often did you have to remind yourself to be kind? What was the impact when you remembered to be kind to yourself?

ACTION: The next time you have an opportunity to show someone kindness, pay close attention to how you deliver this kindness.

REFLECTION: How did you show up? Were you supportive, did you listen, were you empathetic? How do you think paying attention to your delivery affected the other person?

Connection

It's been said that everlasting friends go long periods of time without ever speaking, and never question their friendship. These friends pick up phones like they just spoke yesterday, regardless of how long it has been or how far away they live, and they don't hold grudges. They understand that life is busy and that you will always love them. Share if you have at least 1 of these friends – they will know who they are.

ACTION: Reread the Facebook post from above and notice who springs to mind. Pick up the phone, or write an e-mail to contact them. If they live locally, visit them.

REFLECTION: What happens to the nature of your connection? How does it change based on whether you talk via e-mail, phone or in person? What could you do to enhance the connection?

ACTION: Search for a memory of a place, a person, or an event. Think about it for a while and relive it.

REFLECTION: How does it feel? To what degree do you feel reconnected with that part of your life? How does that make you feel about yourself? What did you learn from reliving that memory?

REFLECTION: Think of a time when you unintentionally made someone feel isolated. What was the circumstance? How quickly did you notice something was wrong? What was the impact on your connection with them? What might help you to recognize such a situation in the future and how could you moderate your approach?

ACTION: Put your new approach into practice. What happens to your connection now?

ACTION: Think about a difficult conversation that you need to have. Develop a strategy that allows you to stay connected with the other person while staying true to the message you want to deliver.

REFLECTION: How did it go? What happened to the quality of your connection with the person both in the moment and over time? What part of your strategy worked best? What would you do differently next time?

REFLECTION: Reflect on times when you are not fully present. What causes you not to be present? How does that affect those around you? What judgments do you have of yourself at these times?

ACTION: Using the information from your reflection, develop a strategy for staying present more often. How did it go? How did that influence the quality of the connection with others?

REFLECTION: Reflect on times when you are fully present. What is different about those situations that allow you to stay present? What does being present feel like?

ACTION: How can you use this information to create a strategy for staying present more often? Practice some more. What did you learn about yourself?

REFLECTION: Reflect on the extent to which you are truly yourself with everyone you know. Who do you mold yourself for? How do you adjust yourself to try to fit in?

ACTION: Take a risk. In the situations that you've identified above, show up as your authentic self. Be who you truly are. What happens? How do you feel about yourself? What happens to your sense of belonging?

Empathy

REFLECTION: Next time you are irritated with someone, try to Pause, Reflect, and Choose (PRC).

   1.   Pause to observe yourself and see how you might be affecting the situation.
   2.   Reflect on what might be going on for the other person and imagine how he or she might feel.
   3.   Choose a different response, one that shows empathy and therefore makes a deposit in your Emotional Bank Account with this person.

ACTION: Practice this over the next week and see how many times you remember to do it. Then notice how many times you choose a different behavior or reaction. How does this influence your relationship with the person? How do you feel about yourself at the end of the week?

REFLECTION: Think back on a conversation that you had recently with someone significant in your life where your lack of empathy put your Emotional Bank Account into the red. How could you have approached the situation differently?

ACTION: Make a deposit in your Emotional Bank Account with that person. How does it affect the quality of your connection with them?

REFLECTION: Reflect on a situation where your own story stood in the way of you showing true empathy for someone. How often does this story influence your interpretation of people and events?

ACTION: Develop a strategy for leaving your story behind and for being completely open to putting yourself in the other person's shoes. What is the result? What is the impact on the other person? How does it affect your Emotional Bank Account with them?

REFLECTION: What situations make you feel defensive, threatened, and protective of yourself, your family, and your friends? How does that affect your ability to show empathy?

ACTION: In the future, try to show empathy with the other person in one of those situations. What did you learn about yourself? Would you do anything differently in the future?

Collaboration

Someone in the Green Zone...	Someone in the Red Zone...
Takes and accept responsibility	Distances from responsibility
Responds non-defensively	Responds defensively
Is not easily threatened	Feels threatened and wronged
Builds mutual success	Triggers defensiveness in others
Seeks solutions not blame	Blames and accuses others
Uses persuasion not force	Creates a climate of antagonism
Is firm, but not rigid	Is rigid, reactive, righteous
Thinks short and long term	Focuses on short term gain/win
Is interested in other perspectives	Feels victimized by different perspectives
Welcomes feedback	Does not seek or value feedback
Sees conflict as natural	Sees conflict as a battle to be won
Talks calmly about difficult issues	Communicates disapproval and contempt
Has a caring attitude	Shows Black/white, right/wrong thinking
Sees excellence over victory	Sees others as the enemy
Listens well	Does not listen well

ACTION: Identify someone with whom you feel safe to ask for feedback on your own collaborative skills. Show them the list of Green Zone and Red Zone behaviors and ask them to tell you how you fare in each category.

REFLECTION: Reflect on their feedback. Was it what you were expecting? What was the biggest surprise? What behavior could you change in order to get better results in future?

REFLECTION: Think of a time when you successfully collaborated as part of a team. What worked well? What challenges did you face? How did you overcome them? What was the end result? What was your contribution to the collaboration?

ACTION: The next time you have the opportunity to collaborate, take the lessons learned from your reflection and apply them. What is the outcome?

REFLECTION: Think of a team or group that you have recently been part of where you were working toward a goal. A team is two or more people. What are the strengths, skills, and experience you bring to the team? Where do you commonly rely on the strengths and skills of others to fill gaps?

ACTION: Write down the list of strengths that you and each of your team members contribute to the success of the team. To what extent are you leveraging everyone's strengths to the fullest? What adjustments can you make in people's roles to increase their contribution? How can you use this strategy for teams that you are part of in the future?

REFLECTION: Think of a situation where you have found it difficult to create a win-win situation. Identify the Green Zone and Red Zone behaviors. How would the outcome have been different if you had a clearer idea of your own interests and the interests of others involved?

ACTION: The next time you are finding collaboration challenging, identify the interests of the other parties. If you don't know what they are, ask. How does understanding their interests affect your problem solving skills? What is the outcome?

REFLECTION: Reflect on the last time you felt yourself getting defensive. What happens? What are your triggers? Devise a strategy for identifying and managing your triggers earlier in the future.

ACTION: When you feel yourself getting defensive, stop. Recall your strategy, and put it into action. What happens to your ability to collaborate? What is the outcome?

Curiosity

REFLECTION: Reflect on the last time you were curious. What did it feel like? What made you open to the experience? How did it impact your relationships?

ACTION: Identify an upcoming situation where you can recreate that feeling of curiosity. It could be something mundane or it could be something that you already expect to be exciting. How does focusing on being curious impact your experience? What did you learn?

REFLECTION: Think of a time when you thought you had a clear view of something and then were disappointed. What you expected was not true; there was ambiguity instead of clarity. How did it make you feel when you thought things were clear? How did it change when it became obvious that the situation was more complex?

ACTION: The next time you find yourself in a situation that seems to be clear, ask yourself a different set of questions to gain a new perspective. Be curious. What happens? What new insights do you gain about yourself, others and the situation?

ACTION: The next time you find yourself resisting trying something new, stop. Draw on your curiosity, let go of your assumptions, and make a different choice.

REFLECTION: How did it feel? What did you learn about yourself? What can you let go of in future? How does this impact you?

ACTION: Identify one of the following situations in which to be more curious.
  - When you meet someone new
  - With someone you don't know very well

Ask questions to understand more about who they are and what is important to them. Share some information about yourself. Listen.

REFLECTION: How did being curious and listening affect your connection with them? Did you identify any resistance or anxiety in yourself about using your curiosity this way? What did you learn about yourself?

REFLECTION: Think of an activity that you have to do so regularly that it has become mundane. The next time you do this activity, re-energize your curiosity. Search for something new in the activity, look for a different perspective. Make notes on your reflection.

ACTION: Talk to someone else about your experience. What new things did you notice? What did you learn about yourself? How did actively practicing curiosity change your experience?

ACTION: The next time you find yourself going down the Judger path, walk yourself through the ABCC process that Adams outlines in *Change Your Questions Change Your Life.*[15];

A – Aware - Am I in Judger?
B – Breathe – Do I need to step back, pause, and look at this situation more objectively?
C – Curiosity – Do I have all the facts? What is happening here?
D – Choice – What's my choice?

REFLECTION: How did going through the above affect the outcome? What did you learn about yourself?

Gratitude

ACTION: For the next week, practice gratitude at least once a day. Try a different approach each time. Complete a journal entry, write a note in your phone, call a friend, and send an email. Identify a way of recording gratitude that is most comfortable for you.

REFLECTION: What did you learn? What felt most comfortable and authentic? What do you think would happen if you practiced gratitude in that way for a week?

ACTION: Using the method of practicing gratitude that you identified in the previous exercise, practice gratitude for a week. In particular, focus on areas of your life or relationships that you want to improve.

REFLECTION: What happened? How did practicing gratitude affect your sense of happiness and well-being? How did it impact your relationships with others?

ACTION: The next time you find yourself frustrated with a situation, pause and reflect. Ask yourself, "What's right about this?" and, "What can I be grateful for?"

REFLECTION: What do you notice? How does choosing to look at a potentially negative situation in this way affect you?

ACTION: The next time you hear of someone else's tragedy, take a moment to count your blessings. Notice your reaction — how reflexive is it to be grateful in that moment? Did you have to remind yourself to be grateful?

REFLECTION: Reflect on how being grateful affects your happiness levels that day and for the next few days. How would practicing gratitude, even when you are not comparing yourself to someone else's misfortune, impact your life? Try it.

REFLECTION: How often do you find yourself feeling grateful but not expressing it or acting on it? What situations hold you back?

ACTION: The next time you're feeling grateful, express it. Explain why, don't just say thank you. Use the opportunity to build a connection. What is the impact on both you and the others involved?

REFLECTION: What gets in the way of gratitude for you? Is it worry, self-judgment, fear, jealousy? Consider why this might be.

ACTION: The next time you experience the feelings you have identified, pull yourself back into the present and count your blessings. How hard is it to do? What is the impact?

Notes

Introduction

1   Anthony Robbins, *Awaken the Giant Within:* How to Take Immediate Control of Your Mental, Emotional, Physical and Financial Destiny! (New York: Free Press, 1991), 32.

2   James W. Tamm and Ronald J. Luyet, *Radical Collaboration: Five Essential Skills to Overcome Defensiveness and Build Successful Relationships (New York: HarperCollins, 2004/2005), 107.* Tamm & Luyet have also developed a workshop called Radical Collaboration® that is offered around the world in 14 languages. For more information about that go to www.RadicalCollaboration.com.

3   Paulo Coelho, *The Pilgrimage* (New York: HarperOne-HarperCollins, 1992), 40-41.

Chapter 1: Freedom

4   Quote attributed to Abraham Lincoln, adapted from his annual message to Congress, December 1, 1862. Quotation found on *Thinkexist.com*, http://thinkexist.com/quotation/freedom_is_the_last-best_hope_of_earth/254892.html.

5   C. Wright Mills, *The Sociological Imagination (New York: Oxford University Press, 1959), 176.*

6   Michael Welp, "Polarity Map Worksheet," *EqualVoice.com,* http://www.equalvoice.com/polrty_map_wrksht.pdf.

7   Marcus Tillius Cicero, original source unknown, found on *BrainyQuote*, http://www.brainyquote.com/quotes/quotes/m/marcustull382338.html.

8   Tamm and Luyet, *Radical Collaboration,* 114.

9   Jim Morrison, original source unknown, found on *QuotationReference. com*, http://www.quotationreference.com/quotefinder.php?byax=1& strt=1&subj=James+Douglas+Morrison.

10   Brené Brown, *The Gifts of Imperfection: Let Go of Who You Think You're Supposed to Be and Embrace Who You Are* (Center City, MN, Hazeldon, 2010), 10-11.

11   Eleanor Roosevelt, original source unknown, found on *The Board of Wisdom*, http://boardofwisdom.com/togo/Quotes/ ShowQuote?msgid=377772#.UjxqfhZzNQM

12   Nelson Mandela, "Nelson Mandela Reflects on Working Toward Peace," original source unknown, essay found at the website of Santa Clara University, The Markkula Center for Applied Ethics, http://www. scu.edu/ethics/architects-of-peace/Mandela/essay.html.

Chapter 2: Impact

13   Jackie Robinson and Alfred Duckett, Epilogue to *I Never Had It Made : An Autobiography of Jackie Robinson* (New York: Ecco, 1972), 268, as quoted on *Wikiquote*, http://en.wikiquote.org/wiki/Jackie_Robinson.

14   Brené Brown, *Daring Greatly: How the Courage to Be Vulnerable Transforms the Way We Live, Love, Parent and Lead (New York: Gotham Books, 2012).*

15   Dalai Lama, original source unknown, found on *Very Best Quotes*, http:// www.verybestquotes.com/everything-you-do-has-some-effect/.

16   Brown, *Daring Greatly, 224.*

17   Charles R. Swindoll, "The Value of a Positive Attitude," *Insight for Living Ministries-www.insight.org,* Jan. 20, 2009, http://daily.insight. org/site/News2?page=NewsArticle&id=13123.

18   Steve Jobs, (commencement address, Stanford University, June, 12, 2005), text available from *Stanford Report,* June 14, 2005, http://news. stanford.edu/news/2005/june15/jobs-061505.html.

19   Brown, *Daring Greatly,* 202.

20   Ibid, 229.

Chapter 3: Kindness

21 Henry James, original source unknown, found at *inagist*, http://inagist.
com/all/377493117928493056/.

22 Tom Rath and Mary Reckmeyer, *How Full is Your Bucket? For Kids* (New
York: Gallup Press, 2009).

23 Anne Herbert as quoted by Adair Lara, "Random Acts of Kindness,"
The San Francisco Chronicle, May, 1991.

24 Sophocles, original source unknown, found on *inagist*, http://inagist.
com/all/377380466850283520/.

25 Lawrence G. Lovasik, *The Hidden Power of Kindness: A Practical
Handbook for Souls Who Dare to Transform the World, One Deed at a
Time (Manchester, NH: Sophia Institute Press, 1962)*, 11.

26 Aesop, *Aesop's Fables*, "The Lion and the Mouse."

27 Piero Ferrucci, *The Power of Kindness: The Unexpected Benefits of
Leading a Compassionate Life,* trans.Vivien Reid Ferrucci (2006; repr.,
New York: Jeremy P. Tarcher-Penguin, 2007), p. 274.

28 Sharon Salzberg, *The Force of Kindness: Change Your Life with Love &
Compassion* (Boulder: Sounds True, 2010), 4.

29 Ibid, 1.

30 Attributed to Mark Twain, original source unknown, found at
marktwain: All About Mark Twain, July 8, 2013, http://aboutmarktwain.
com/206/2013/07/08/kindness-is-a-language-that-the-deaf-can-hear-
and-the-blind-can-see-mark-twain/.

31 Ferrucci, *The Power of Kindness, 128.*

32 Salzberg, *The Force of Kindness, 89-90.*

33 Ibid, 96.

Chapter 4: Connection

34 John Donne, "Meditation XVII," *Devotions upon Emergent Occasions,*
1624.

35 Lois Wyse, original source unknown, found at *Thinkexist.com,* http://
thinkexist.com/quotation/a-good-friend-is-a-connection-to-life-a-
tie-to/348586.html.

36 Helen Keller, orginal source unknown, found at *BrainyQuote,* http://
www.brainyquote.com/quotes/quotes/h/helenkelle386647.html.

37 Harriet Lerner, prologue to *The Dance of Connection: How to Talk to Someone When You're Mad, Hurt, Scared, Frustrated, Insulted, Betrayed, or Desperate* (New York: HarperCollins, 2001) xii.

38 Ibid, 74.

39 Ibid, 60.

40 Eckhart Tolle, *Practicing The Power of Now: Essential Teachings, Meditations, and Exercises from the Power of Now* (Novato, CA: New World Library, 1999), 30.

41 Brown, *Daring Greatly,* 137.

42 Coelho, *The Pilgrimage,* 43.

43 Brown, *Daring Greatly, 145.*

44 Pearl Bailey, original source unknown, found at *BrainyQuote,* http://www.brainyquote.com/quotes/quotes/p/pearlbaile383199.html .

45 Brown, *Daring Greatly, 145.*

46 Ibid, 145-146.

47 Ibid, 81.

Chapter 5: Empathy

48 Alfred Adler, original source unknown, found at *goodreads*, http://www.goodreads.com/quotes/776552-seeing-with-the-eyes-of-another-listening-with-the-ears .

49 Stephen R. Covey, *The 7 Habits of Highly Effective People: Restoring the Character Ethic* (New York: Fireside-Simon & Schuster, 1989), 188.

50 Ian McEwan, "Only love and then oblivion. Love was all they had to set against their murderers," *The Guardian*, September 15, 2001, www.theguardian.com/world/2001/sep/15/september11.politicsphilosophyandsociety2.

51 Meryl Streep, original source unknown, found at *goodreads*, http://www.goodreads.com/quotes/83963-the-great-gift-of-human-beings-is-that-we-have.

52 Brown, *Daring Greatly,* 81.

53 Covey, *The 7 Habits of Highly Effective People,* 242.

54 Ibid, 245.

55 Ibid, 190.

56 David Brooks, "The Limits of Empathy," *The New York Times*, September 29, 2011.

57   Covey, *The 7 Habits of Highly Effective People,* 241.

58   Ibid, 238.

Chapter 6: Collaboration

59   Henry Ford, source unknown, found at *BrainyQuote,* http://www.
      brainyquote.com/quotes/quotes/h/henryford121997.html.

60   Tamm and Luyet, *Radical Collaboration,* 27.

61   Ryunosuke Satoro, original source unknown, found at *BrainyQuote,*
      http://www.brainyquote.com/quotes/authors/r/ryunosuke_satoro.
      html.

62   Bruce Tuckman, "Developmental Sequence in Small Groups,"
      Psychological Bulletin 63, no. 6 (1965): 384-99.

63   Tamm and Luyet, *Radical Collaboration,* 4.

64   Ibid, *9.*

65   Kenneth W. Thomas and Ralph H. Kilmann, "Thomas-Kilmann Conflict
      Mode Instrument (TKI)" (Mountain View, CA: CPP).

66   Xan Brooks, "London 2012 Olympics opening ceremony – as it happened:
      Seven small sparks, one great flame," *The Guardian,* July 27, 2012, http://
      www.theguardian.com/sport/london-2012-olympics-blog/2012/
      jul/27/london-2012-olympics-opening-ceremony-live.

67   Lord Sebastian Coe's speech at the London 2012 Olympic Games
      Opening Ceremony, "The Games of the XXX Olympiad," National
      Broadcasting Co., July 27, 2012.

68   African proverb quoted by Al Gore, posted by Matt in "Principle: If You
      Want to Go Fast, Go Alone. If You Want to Go Far, Go Together, *"Media
      Shelf (blog),* April 11, 2011, http://yourmediashelf.com/2011/04/
      principle-if-you-want-to-go-fast-go-alone-if-you-want-to-go-far-go-
      together.

69   Phil Jackson, original source unknown, found at *goodreads,* http://
      www.goodreads.com/quotes/527132-the-strength-of-the-team-is-
      each-individual-member-the.

70   Douglas B. Reeves, *Transforming Professional Development into
      Student Results* (Alexandria, VA: ASCD, 2010), p. 50.

71   Tamm & Luyet, *Radical Collaboration,* 202.

72   Ibid, 206.

73   Ibid, 167.

74 Jack R. Gibb, "Defensive Communication" *Journal of Communication 11*, no. 3, (September 1961): 141 -148. Article first published online: February, 7 2006, doi: 10.1111/j.1460-2466.1961.tb00344.x

75 Enrico Casarosa, interviewed by Jim Macquarrie, "La Luna, The Short Before Pixar's *Brave,* Is a Homage to Family," *Wired,* June 13, 2012, http://www.wired.com/geekdad/2012/06/la-luna-enrico-casarosa/.

76 Tamm & Luyet, *Radical Collaboration, 28.*

Chapter 7: Curiosity

77 Arnold Edinborough, original source unknown, found at *Thinkexist. com,* http://thinkexist.com/quotation/curiosity_is_the_very_basis_of_education_and_if/264586.html

78 Todd Kashdan, *Curious: Discover the Missing Ingredient to a Fulfilling Life* (New York: William Morrow, 2009), 11.

79 Marilee Adams, *Change Your Questions, Change Your Life: 10 Powerful Tools for Life and Work, 2nd ed.* (San Francisco: Berrett-Koehler, 2009), 38-39.

80 Ibid, 36.

81 Smiley Blanton, original source unknown, found at *The Quotations Page,* http://www.quotationspage.com/quotes/Dr._Smiley_Blanton/.

82 Kashdan, *Curious,* 23.

83 Ibid, 7.

84 Albert Einstein statement to William Miller, as quoted in *Life Magazine,* May 2, 1955.

85 Tony Schwartz, "Turning 60: The Twelve Most Important Lessons I've Learned So Far," *The Harvard Business Review Blog Network,* May 1, 2012, http://blogs.hbr.org/2012/05/turning-60-the-twelve-most/.

86 Penelope Lively, original source unknown, found at BrainyQuote, http://www.brainyquote.com/quotes/quotes/p/penelopeli222861.html.

87 Kashdan, *Curious,* 39.

88 Ibid, 240.

89 Ibid, 89.

90 Ibid, 71.

91 Anonymous, original source unknown, found at *LifeQuotesLib. com*, "Anonymous Quotes," http://www.lifequoteslib.com/authors/ anonymous_61.html

92 Ibid, 174.

93 Adams, *Change Your Questions, 124.*

94 Ibid, 37.

95 Ibid, 94.

96 Kashdan, *Curious,* 19.

97 Ibid, 2.

Chapter 8: Gratitude

98 Meister Eckhart, original source unknown, found at *BrainyQuote, http://www.brainyquote.com/quotes/quotes/m/meistereck149158. html.*

99 M.J. Ryan, *Attitudes of Gratitude: How to Give and Receive Joy Every Day of Your Life;* 10th Anniversary ed. (1999, repr., San Francisco: Red Wheel/Weiser, 2009), 14.

100 Brother David Steindl-Rast, *Gratefulness, the Heart of Prayer: An Approach to Life in Fullness,* (Mahwah, NJ: Paulist Press, 1990), 213.

101 Ryan, *Attitudes of Gratitude,* 122.

102 Sonja Lyubomirsky, *The How of Happiness: A New Approach to Getting the Life You Want* (New York: Penguin, 2007), 89.

103 Martin Seligman, *Flourish: A Visionary New Understanding of Happiness and Well-being* (New York: Free Press, 2011), 30.

104 Ursula K. Le Guin, *The Left Hand of Darkness,* (1969; repr., New York: Ace Books, 1987), 220 . Citation refers to Ace mass market paperback edition.

105 Ryan, *Attitudes of Gratitude,* 28.

106 Ibid, 116.

107 William Arthur Ward, original source unknown, found at *BrainyQuote, http://www.brainyquote.com/quotes/quotes/w/williamart105516. html.*

108 Ryan, *Attitudes of Gratitude,* 74.

109 Eric Hoffer, *Reflections on the Human Condition* (Titusville, NJ: Hopewell Publications, 1973), Section 172, as quoted on *Wikiquote,* http://en.wikiquote.org/wiki/Eric_Hoffer.

110 Ryan, *Attitudes of Gratitude,* 27

111 Alex Korb, "The Grateful Brain: The neuroscience of giving thanks," *Prefrontal Nudity: The Brain Exposed (blog), Psychology Today, November 20, 2012, http://www.psychologytoday.com/blog/ prefrontal-nudity/201211/the-grateful-brain.*

112 Lyubomirsky, *The How of Happiness, 89.*